Zen Antics

ALSO BY THOMAS CLEARY

The Blue Cliff Record (1977, 1992)*
The Flower Ornament Scripture (1984–1987, 1993)*
Shōbōgenzō: Zen Essays of Dōgen (1986)
Zen Essence: The Science of Freedom (1989)*
Zen Lessons: The Art of Leadership (1989)*
Transmission of Light, by Zen Master Keizan (1990)
No Barrier, by Mumon (1993)
Rational Zen: The Mind of Dōgen Zenji (1993)*

* Published by Shambhala Publications

Zen Antics

○ ○ ○ ○ ○

A Hundred Stories
of Enlightenment

○ ○ ○ ○

Translated and edited by
Thomas Cleary

○ ○ ○

○ ○

○

Shambhala
Boston & London
1993

Shambhala Publications, Inc.
Horticultural Hall
300 Massachusetts Avenue
Boston, Massachusetts 02115

9 8 7 6 5 4 3 2 1

First Edition
Printed in the United States of America on acid-free paper ♾
Distributed in the United States by Random House, Inc.,
and in Canada by Random House of Canada Ltd

Library of Congress Cataloging-in-Publication Data

Cleary, Thomas F., 1949–
    Zen antics: 100 stories of enlightenment/translated from the Japanese by
Thomas Cleary.—1st ed.
        p.   cm.
    ISBN 0-87773-944-7 (acid-free paper)
    1. Zen Buddhism—Anecdotes.   2. Enlightenment (Zen Buddhism)—
Anecdotes.   I. Title.
BQ9265.8.C54   1993   93-12213
294.3′44—dc20   CIP

Contents

Translator's Introduction

Zen Buddhism is a science of awakening the mind, an art of spiritual enlightenment. Once practiced throughout East Asia in a wide variety of forms by people from many cultures and walks of life, Zen is not a body of dogma but a way of clarifying and enchancing consciousness.

Zen is called "a special transmission outside of doctrine, not defined by literal formulations, but directly pointing to the human mind for the perception of its essence and fulfillment of enlightenment." Anciently known as the school of the enlightened heart, the gateway to the source, and the unalloyed communication of mind by mind, Zen absorbed and pervaded the vast spectrum of Buddhist practices and teachings, while concentrating on the keys to their practical realization.

All Buddhist teachings are concerned with either or both of the two fundamental facets of Buddhism, self-help and helping others, wisdom and compassion. These two phases of Buddhism are carried out by means of practices implementing what are known as the six and ten perfections or transcendent ways.

The significance of these formats may be kept in mind by means of a play on the original Sanskrit word for the perfections, *pāramitā,* which literally means "having reached the goal," or "having gone beyond." In essence, the *pāramitās* may be called the *parameters* of Buddhism, the characteristic values underlying all Buddhist systems.

The phase of self-help in Buddhism is characterized by the six *pāramitās* of giving, discipline, patience, energy, meditation, and insight.

Three main kinds of giving are traditionally defined in Buddhism: giving material support; giving security; and giving education. Giving also means relinquishment, non-attachment.

There are also three main kinds of discipline traditionally defined: the discipline of restraining evil; the discipline of constructive virtue; and the discipline associated with concentration. Zen also teaches formless discipline of mind.

Many kinds of patience are practiced in Buddhism, including the patience involved in tolerating disdain and abuse; the patience involved in tolerating painful truths; and the patience needed to accept ultimate truth.

Energy refers to the perseverance and spiritual heroism needed to break through the boundaries of conditioning, free the mind from needless limitations of habit, and fulfill its potential.

Meditation is needed to gather and focus attention to a depth and degree sufficient to enable the practitioner to alter perception and experience of self and world at will. The science of meditation is elaborated and perfected to a rare degree in Buddhism, with innumerable methods designed to accommodate the needs of people of all sorts of potentials and capacities.

Insight commonly refers to a special kind of knowledge in Buddhism, a precognitive or intuitive sense of the essence of things, functioning spontaneously and instantaneously without the intervention of linear reasoning. This enables the whole mind to operate at a higher level of objectivity and integrity, freeing the individual from delusion.

There are countless variations on the practices of the six *pāramitās*, depending on the needs of the individual concerned. In every case, however, they have to be combined in order to produce the desired effect. Thus while the six *pāramitās* may be viewed as a series in some sense, they are more properly understood as a set, which may be depicted in a circle. In the early stages of practice, the six perfections may be viewed as functioning in complementary pairs.

Eventually the practices and realizations of each and every

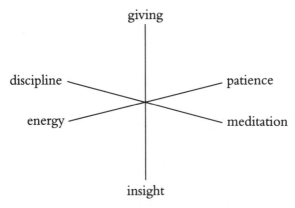

giving

discipline   patience

energy   meditation

insight

one of the six *pāramitās* integrate with those of all the others, complementing and perfecting them. In Zen lore, the opening of insight is often referred to as awakening or enlightenment, but this only signals a stage at which higher integration of the six *pāramitās* may commence in real experience, not the supreme perfect enlightenment of which Buddhist scriptures speak.

That supreme perfect enlightenment is realized through a more advanced program of ten *pāramitās*, which goes on to develop the capacity to attain not only sufficient enlightenment for oneself but the greater enlightenment to liberate others.

The ten *pāramitās* include the foregoing six, adding to them four higher perfections of increasing sophistication, known as skill in means, vowing, power, and knowledge.

Skill in means refers to the ability to devise and employ appropriate techniques to liberate and enlighten other people. Buddhism evolved countless such expedient means over the centuries in order to accommodate the needs and potentials of all sorts of individual and collective psychological types in every phase of human civilization.

Vowing, or commitment, is the use of directed will for the purpose of linking the individual consciousness with the totality of Buddhism, joining self-development and the welfare of others in an inseparable continuity. Many typical vows of welfare, liberation, and enlightenment are described in Buddhist literature, but all of them are based on the same fundamental principles.

Power refers to the awakening of higher capacities and spiritual gifts for the purpose of empowering the operation of the total dynamic of the ten *pāramitās*. While these capacities are believed to be inherent in all people and these gifts are believed to derive from a universal endowment, nevertheless they are also believed to be veiled in the world by delusions and attachments, and therefore only really useful in concert with the actual practice of the other nine *pāramitās*.

Knowledge, as the tenth *pāramitā* of Buddhism, is of a scope whose vastness is such that it can scarcely be defined in all of its particulars and ramifications. Included therein is knowledge of all the arts and sciences of wakefulness, self-understanding, and freedom; of perceiving and distinguishing absolute, relative, and conventional truths; of harmonizing intuition, imagination, and reason; and of purposeful living and meaningful action, with the ability to adapt to any and all circumstances.

Because of their cooperative functions within a totally integrated dynamic, it is also convenient to represent the ten *pāramitās* as a circle or sphere. Here again, the practical application of the ten *pāramitās* may be visualized as beginning with the complementary pairs on opposite ends of five diameters or planes and reaching perfection with the full interpenetration of all ten *pāramitās*.

Because of the infinite richness and complexity of the experience of the ten *pāramitās*, innumerable methods of teaching and integrating them were developed. Among its many techniques, Zen is particularly known for its use of highly concentrated stories to stamp the mind with impressions of the ten *pāramitās*, inductively leading the seeker to a rounded and integrated vision and experience of their total dynamic.

These stories are not necessarily history as conventionally conceived. Like all history, most of the history of Zen is really unrecorded in books, and there is no way of getting around this fact by conventional historiography. The real purpose of Zen stories is not in documenting events of the past, but in their effect on their reader, and so this is their real history.

These stories are also most definitely not representations of role models, as this term is currently understood. The figures in the stories come from worlds that no longer exist, so they have no value as role models in a contemporary sense.

The principles and practices they represent, however—the ten *pāramitās* of Buddhism—do exist and can be put into effect. They have to be realized and applied today as always, here as anywhere, in a manner suited to the particular conditions and needs of the time, place, and people concerned.

Zen Antics

The Temple Gate

Once there was a wealthy man, Hei-zayemon by name, who strove to realize in his life the virtues commended by ancient sages.

An earnest and studious man, Hei-zayemon used to spend liberally of his wealth in acts of benevolence, charity, and welfare.

Many infants of impoverished families were rescued by his intervention, and he personally financed the construction of numerous bridges and roads in his province for the convenience of the people.

When he died, Hei-zayemon stipulated in his will that his bequest should be used to continue relief work through the generations, and this was honored by his children and grandchildren.

One day, they say, there appeared at the door of Hei-zayemon a certain Buddhist friar. It seems that this clergyman had heard of the wealthy man's selfless benevolence, unusual among the rich of his time, and had come to ask him for money to build a temple gate.

The philanthropist laughed in the friar's face and said, "I help people because I cannot bear to see them suffer. What's so bad about a temple without a gate?"

The Teacher of the High Priest

Once upon a time there was a certain high priest of a Zen sect whose patron was none other than the baron of a province. When he went to the capital city to visit the baron at his official residence, therefore, the high priest would travel in style, with a large retinue and much fanfare.

It happened on one such journey that the horsemen wanted to purchase some new footwear at a certain way station where the entourage had stopped to rest. An old man was called in at the recommendation of the local porters, who said that he made very good straw sandals.

Now when this old man came over with some new sandals for the horsemen, the high priest saw him through the window of his palanquin and nearly fainted.

The old sandal maker was none other than Tōsui, the illuminated Zen master who had been his own teacher many years earlier, before a mysterious disappearance from his temple.

Tumbling out of his carriage in shock and embarrassment, the high priest prostrated himself before the old man and paid his respects with utmost courtesy.

Tōsui was kind to him and spoke of old times; but when they parted, the master said to the priest, "Don't let yourself become intoxicated by association with nobles."

Cleanliness of Heart

Once a group of beggars afflicted with leprosy came to the assembly of Zen master Bankei, a great-hearted teacher of the masses. Bankei admitted them to his company, and when he initiated them, he even washed and shaved their heads with his own hands.

Now as it happened, there was a certain gentleman present, the representative of a baron who had faith in Bankei and had already built a temple in his province where the teacher could train disciples and lecture to the people.

Revolted by the sight of the Zen master shaving the heads of untouchables, the gentleman hurriedly brought a basin of water for Bankei to wash his hands.

But the master refused, remarking, "Your disgust is filthier than their sores."

The Old Tea Seller

Once there was an old man who used to run a floating outdoor tea room in the scenic environs of Kyoto, the ancient imperial capital of Japan.

In spring he would search out the places where the flowers were most beautiful, and in autumn he would find the areas where the foliage was best; there he would bring out his tea utensils and set up seats to wait on hikers enjoying the sights.

The aesthetes of Kyoto were delighted and used to gather around wherever he set up shop. Before long the Old Tea Seller became widely known in the capital.

Few people knew that the old man was a hidden Zen master. A student of Zen since boyhood, he had visited Buddhist teachers all over the country. Traveling constantly, he had no material possessions, being entirely devoted to the study of Buddhism.

After realizing Zen awakening, he had undertaken a commitment to perpetual study and self-refinement, in order to avoid straying from the path to complete enlightenment by premature assumption of authority.

After his extensive travels, the master returned to his native place to help his original Zen teacher. When the teacher died, the master nominated one of the disciples to inherit the abbacy.

He himself disappeared and went to Kyoto, leaving ecclesiastic office behind forever. At that time, he said, "Whether one's livelihood is correct is a matter of mind, not appearances. I do not wish to take advantage of monk's robes to live on alms at others' expense."

Thus he began to sell tea to support himself. He used to jokingly tell people, "I'm poor and can't afford to eat meat,

I'm old and can't please a wife. The livelihood of a tea seller is suitable for me."

Eventually the master burned all his tea paraphernalia and retired.

Finally he died in a hermitage in the year 1763, at the age of eighty-nine.

When he set up shop, the old man used to hang out this sign:

"The price of tea is however much you give me, from a hundred pounds of gold to half a penny. You can even drink for free, if you like; but I can't give you a better bargain than that."

When he ultimately burned his utensils and retired, these were his words to his carrying basket:

"I have always been alone and poor, with neither a patch of ground nor a hoe. You have helped me for many a year, accompanying me to the spring mountains and autumn rivers, selling tea under the pines and in the shade of bamboo groves. Thus I have not lacked money for meals and have lasted for over eighty years.

"But now I am so old that I haven't the strength to use you any more. Hiding my body in the North Star, I am about to end my days. Lest you be disgraced in the future by mundane hands, I reward you with the Trance of Fire: now be transformed in the midst of the flames.

"How can we express this transformation? The conflagration ending the aeon clear, everything is consumed; yet the green mountains are there as ever in the white clouds. Now I consign you to the spirit of fire."

Economy

Sōkai was so poor that he owned no clothing but a single robe, which he wore all year round, in all weather.

One summer day, Sōkai washed his robe and hung it in a tree to dry. In the meantime, while waiting for his robe to dry out, he went to sit in the graveyard behind the temple, stark naked.

As it happened, the lord of the province paid a visit to the grave of his father, in that very graveyard, on that very day. Needless to say, he was quite taken aback to see a naked monk sitting there among the tombs.

When the lord asked him what he was doing, Sōkai explained the situation truthfully. Moved by his candor, the lord had a set of clothing made for him. Later on, when Sōkai had become a Zen teacher, the lord became his disciple.

Zen in Government

One day the governor of a certain province asked Zen master Shōsan about the essentials of Buddhism.

The master told him, "It is essential for you to encompass the whole province, in its complete totality. You cannot do this if you are wishy-washy. Be keenly attentive in every way, and make your official decisions with kindness and compassion.

"Then, forging right ahead, you should clearly distinguish people's natures and get to know them. Generally speaking, if a leader is narrow-minded and cannot distinguish people's natures, he will find a lot of things offensive. Then his mood goes out and fights with the moods of others. Is that not stupid?"

Studying Mind

Mind Studies was a lay self-improvement movement influenced by Zen. One day a follower of Mind Studies came to Zen master Shōsan to ask about the essentials of Buddhism.

The Zen master said, "Buddhism is not a matter of using your discursive intellect to govern your body. It is a matter of using the moment of the immediate present purely, not wasting it, without thinking about past or future.

"This is why the ancients exhorted people first of all to be careful of time: this means guarding the mind strictly, sweeping away all things, whether good or bad, and detaching from the ego.

"Furthermore," the Zen master continued, "for the reformation of mind it is good to observe the principle of cause and effect. For example, even if others hate us, we should not resent them; we should criticize ourselves, thinking why people should hate us for no reason, assuming that there must be a causal factor in us, and even that there must be other as yet unknown causal factors in us.

"Maintaining that all things are effects of causes, we should not make judgments based on subjective ideas. On the whole, things do not happen in accord with subjective ideas; they happen in accord with the laws of Nature. If you maintain awareness of this, your mind will become very clear."

Indifference

National Teacher Daitō Kokushi, whose honorific name means "Great Lamp, Teacher of the Nation," was one of the founders of the renowned Ō-Tō-Kan school of Rinzai Zen. He died in the fourteenth century.

According to the custom of ancient Zen schools, Daitō disappeared from the monastery after his enlightenment, to mature his realization hidden in the midst of the world.

It was not until years later that he was discovered living under a bridge in Kyoto, in the society of homeless beggars. From there he became a teacher of the emperor.

Daitō once wrote a poem about his life as an outcast:

When one sits in meditation,
one sees the people
coming and going
over the avenue bridge
as trees growing deep in the mountains.

Objectivity

The Zen master Tenkei was considered one of the eight greatest Buddhist adepts of his time. Master of all schools, Tenkei helped revive Zen in the early 1700s through his many enlightened disciples and his many written works in classical and contemporary modes.

Once Tenkei quoted the famous poem of National Teacher Daitō and offered one of his own:

When one sits in meditation,
one sees the people
coming and going
over the avenue bridge
just as they are.

Zen and the Art of Government

A certain lord used to call on Zen master Tenkei to ask about the essence of Buddhism. When the master was in his last illness, the lord sent a messenger to ask after him. Tenkei sent the messenger back to the lord with this note:

"To manage a household and to govern a state are also religious practices. Be careful to implement humane policies, so that there is trust and harmony between the ruler and the ruled. This is my last advice."

Wiping a Buddha's Ass

In Zen master Hakuin's group there was a crazy monk who thought he had realized the identity of self and Buddha. He tore up Buddhist scriptures and used the pages for toilet paper.

Other monks took him to task for this, but he paid no attention, haughtily retorting, "What's wrong with using Buddhist scriptures to wipe a Buddha's ass?"

Now someone repeated this to the master Hakuin, who asked the crazy monk, "They say you are using Buddhist scriptures for toilet paper. Is that so?"

The crazy monk said, "Yes. I myself am a Buddha. What is wrong with using Buddhist scriptures to wipe a Buddha's ass?"

Hakuin said, "You're wrong. Since it's a Buddha's ass, why use old paper with writing on it? You should wipe it with clean white paper."

The crazy monk was shamed, and he apologized.

Conduct

A monk asked Zen master Bankei, "Is it not harmless to joke around in spontaneous moments of levity?"

Bankei said, "It's all right if you want to lose trust."

Mind Art

A certain lord came to ask master Bankei about the Zen "mind art." Instead of welcoming his inquiry, Bankei upbraided the lord, saying, "I understand you dismissed a secular scholar because you did not recognize his worthiness. How can you even ask about the Zen mind art?"

An Awakening

Zen master Setsugen told his student Jijō, "If you meditate single-mindedly without interruption for seven days and nights and yet still do not attain realization, you can cut off my head and make my skull into a nightsoil scoop."

Not long after that, Jijō came down with a case of dysentery. Taking a bucket to a secluded place, he sat on it and held his attention in right mindfulness.

When he had sat on the bucket for seven straight days, one night he suddenly sensed the whole world like a snowy landscape under bright moonlight and felt as if the entire universe were too small to contain him.

He had been absorbed in this state for a long time when he was startled into self-awareness on hearing a sound. He found his whole body running with sweat, and his sickness had disappeared. In celebration he wrote a verse:

> *Radiant, spiritual—what is this?*
> *The minute you blink your eyes you've missed it.*
> *The spatula by the toilet shines with light;*
> *After all it was just me all along.*

The Ultimate Point

The Zen priest Taigu was requested to become the abbot of a temple. A local woman who had lost a child came to ask the new abbot to perform the funerary rites.

The woman said to the Zen priest, "I would consider myself fortunate to be favored with your compassion. Please tell me where my child has gone."

Taigu couldn't answer. The woman left, weeping bitterly.

The Zen priest said to himself, "I thought I had attained realization. This woman's question has shown me I don't know the ultimate point. What is the purpose of being an abbot in a temple?"

So Taigu gave up his position and departed, seeking to deepen his understanding of Zen.

Gut

A certain lord who studied Zen from Bankei was young and fond of martial arts. One day he decided to test the master's "gut" by suddenly attacking him with a lance as his sat quietly.

The Zen master calmly deflected the thrust with his rosary. Then he said to the lord, "Your technique is still immature; your mind moved first."

"Don't Be Disturbed"

Mugaku was one of the founders of Zen in Japan. Born in China, he experienced his first awakening at the age of twelve, when he heard a Zen verse while visiting a country temple with his father:

> Bamboo shadows sweep the stairs,
> yet not a mote of dust is stirred;
> Moonlight pierces the depths of the pond,
> leaving no trace in the water.

When the Mongol horde of Kublai Khan broke into southern China in 1275, Mugaku fled the fires of battle; but when the province where he had taken refuge was overrun the next year, he stopped running away.

As the Mongol warriors stormed the monastic compound where Mugaku sat, all the other Chinese monks and monastic workers concealed themselves like mice in their burrows.

The warriors drew near to the Zen master sitting alone in the hall and put their swords to his neck. Thoroughly composed, Mugaku calmly chanted a verse:

> In all the universe, I haven't even
> ground enough to stand a single cane;
> Lucky it is that I've found
> personality void and phenomena empty.
> Farewell, swords of the Mongol empire.

Moved by the fearless composure of the Zen master, the Mongol soldiers put up their swords and left.

In the year 1280, Mugaku was invited to Japan by Hōjō Tokimune, regent for the shogun. When Tokimune visited the Zen master in the spring of the following year, Mugaku wrote the regent a three-word message: "Don't be disturbed."

When Tokimune asked for an explanation, the Zen master said, "At the junction of spring and summer, southern Japan will be in an uproar; but it will settle down before long, so you should not worry."

As it turned out, a Mongol invasion force attacked southern Japan that very autumn, just as the Zen master had said. And as the master predicted, the invaders were repelled and peace was soon restored.

Winning without Trying

The Way of Winning without Trying was a school of martial arts founded by a warrior named Tsukahara Bokuden. A famous story about him illustrates the name and methodology of his school.

Once in the course of a journey to eastern Japan, Bokuden took passage across a bay on a small boat carrying five or six other passengers.

During the trip over the water, all of the passengers sat quietly except for a big, burly man who kept talking in a loud voice, bragging about his peerless powers in martial arts.

At first, Bokuden tried to snooze, paying no attention to the ruffian. At length, however, weary of the man's boasting, Bokuden turned to him and said, "Well, now we've heard all sorts of stories from you, haven't we? What I don't understand in them are the tall tales about martial arts. I myself have practiced martial arts since youth, exercising according to the established forms, but up until now I have never thought of trying to beat anyone. All I have worked on is how to avoid losing to anyone."

Hearing this, the brash man asked, "What school of martial arts do you follow?"

Bokuden replied, "Winning without Trying, or the Way of Not Losing."

The man retorted, "If it is a matter of winning without trying, why are you armed with swords?"

Bokuden answered, "The two swords of 'communicating mind by mind' break the point of conceit and cut off the sprouts of wrong thoughts."

Hearing this, the ruffian challenged Bokuden to a contest, saying, "Then if we have a duel, will you win without trying?"

Bokuden said, "In this case, although the sword of my heart is a life-giving sword, insofar as the opponent is a bad man, it becomes a death-dealing sword."

Now the arrogant man could no longer contain his mounting anger. He ordered the boatman to make for shore at once so that he and Bokuden could have it out.

Bokuden surreptitiously signaled to the boatman with his eyes, then said to the braggart, "The shoreline is a busy port, too crowded for a duel. I'll show you the Way of

Winning without Trying By Not Losing, over yonder, on that islet off the promontory up ahead. Although I'm sure the other people on this boat are in a hurry to be on their way, if you insist so much, we might as well have a duel."

So the boatman rowed up to an islet, whereupon the ruffian leaped out onto the shore, drawing his long sword. He shouted at Bokuden, "Come on, come on! I'll split your face in two!"

Still aboard the boat, Bokuden replied, "Wait a minute. The Way of Winning without Trying requires one to calm the mind." So saying, Bokuden removed his swords from his belt and handed them to the boatman, taking up in exchange the boatman's pole.

For a moment it looked like Bokuden was going to beach the boat on the shore; then all at once he thrust the pole in the opposite direction and pushed the boat out into the water.

Seeing this, the ruffian shouted, "Why don't you come up here onto the shore?"

Bokuden said with a laugh, "Why should I? If you have a complaint, then swim out here, and I'll give you a lesson for the road. This is the Way of Winning without Trying!"

A Zen Retreat

Zen master Taigu lived for a time deep in the mountains in the provincial countryside north of Kyoto. He wrote a pair of verses commemorating this abode:

> *No more city troubles,*
> *No contests of judgment:*
> *In autumn I sweep*
> *the leaves by the stream,*
> *In spring I hear*
> *the birds in the trees.*

Spring comes to the human world
with vast and great kindness;
Every flower blossom
holds forth a Buddha.
Unawares, remaining snow
has melted all away—
Myriad forms unfurl their brows
in concert, all as one.

The Founding of a Temple

When Zen master Taigu went to the capital city of Edo in the midseventeenth century, the shogun himself, Tokugawa Iemitsu, expressed his wish for an audience with the Zen master.

Taigu disappeared the very night he was summoned to see the shogun. He was not heard of again for ten years.

One autumn, Taigu went on a journey to bathe in the hot springs of a certain province, in order to treat his arthritis. Taking the road through Snow Country, the Zen master spent the winter as a guest in the house of a pious lay Buddhist.

As it happened, the distinguished Zen master Gudō, who was an old friend of Taigu, also came to visit the very same house.

Now when the governor of the province heard of the presence of these two great Zen elders in his domain, he invited them to his mansion to talk about the Teaching.

Being arthritic and stiff in both legs, Taigu used to sit on a thick cushion. When he and Gudō were ushered into the reception room at the governor's mansion, to their surprise the governor himself placed a thick cushion on the seat for Taigu, perceiving his infirmity and treating him with great consideration.

Gudō remarked, "Governor, you are very perceptive, but I'm afraid you won't live long."

Taigu became red in the face and said, "This old fellow Gudō doesn't know good from bad—he approves people at random. What does an immature youth know?"

The governor praised Taigu, saying, "He is genuinely fit to be a teacher."

As a result of this meeting, the governor had a temple built and made Taigu the first master there.

Teaching Zen

One day the governor of the province asked Zen master Taigu, "They say *The Blue Cliff Record* is the foremost of Zen books: Is this true?"

Taigu said, "It is."

The governor requested, "Please expound one or two stories from that book."

Taigu said, "I'm afraid you wouldn't understand."

But the governor kept begging, so finally Taigu said loudly, quoting the first story of that Zen book. " 'Being empty, there is no holiness.' "

The governor said, "I don't understand."

Taigu said, "After all you couldn't hold steady."

The Passing of a Master

The illustrious Zen master Bankei died in a country temple in the last decade of the seventeenth century. At the end, his disciples asked him for a parting verse, according to the ancient Zen custom.

The master said, "I have been in this world for seventy-three years, of which I have spent forty-four teaching Zen to liberate others. All that I have pointed out to you in over half a lifetime is my parting verse. There is no other parting verse to compose. Why should I imitate everyone else and make a confession on my deathbed?"

Having said this, the great Zen master Bankei passed away, sitting perfectly straight.

A Lone Lamp

Sonome was a well known poetess and a profound student of Buddhism. She once wrote to Zen master Unkō: "To seek neither reality nor falsehood is the root source of the Great Way. Everyone knows this, so even though I may seem immodest for saying so, I do not think this is anything special. As goings-on in the source of one mind, the willows are green, the flowers are red. Just being as is, I pass the time reciting verse and composing poetry. If this is useless chatter, then the scriptures are also useless chatter. I dislike anything that stinks of religion, and my daily practice is invocation, poetry, and song. If I go to paradise, that's fine; if I fall into hell, that's auspicious."

> By myself I remember
> not to seek mind;
> the green lamp has already illumined
> my lone lamp heart.
> Whether in clamor or silence,
> I have a clear mirror:
> it thoroughly discerns
> pure hearts among humans.
>
> It is not something existing,
> that anyone can see and know,
> nor does it not exist:
> such is the lamp of truth.

When Sonome was about to pass on, she bade farewell to the world with this poem:

The sky of the autumn moon
and the warmth of spring:
Is it a dream? Is it real?
Hail to the Buddha of Infinite Light!

Better than Flowers

One spring the haiku poet Bashō decided to take a trip to see the flowers in a certain place famed for its scenery. Along the way he heard of a poor peasant girl noted for devotion to her parents. Intrigued, Bashō went looking for the girl. When he found her, he gave her all the money he had brought for his travel expenses. Then he returned home, without having seen the flowers.

He said, "This year I have seen something better than flowers."

Communication

Once when Zen master Bankei was about to leave a temple in the capital where he taught from time to time, a certain gentleman came requesting that the master pospone his departure. A certain baron had a question and wanted to see the Zen master in person on the morrow to resolve it. Bankei assented and put off leaving.

The next day, however, the gentleman came again, this time with the message that the baron had some urgent business to take care of and could not come to see the master. The baron had asked the gentleman to relay his question to Bankei, then report the Zen master's answer back to him.

When he had heard the gentleman out, Bankei said, "This matter of Zen is difficult to convey even by direct question and direct answer; it is all the more difficult to convey by messenger."

The Zen master said nothing more. Speechless, the gentleman withdrew and departed.

Reality

Zen master Tenkei used to admonish his followers, "You should be genuine in all things. Nothing that is genuine in the world is not genuine in Buddhism, and nothing that is not genuine in Buddhism is genuine in the world."

He would also say, "See with your eyes, hear with your ears. Nothing in the world is hidden; what would you have me say?"

A Healing Buddha

Tomomura Yūshōshi, "Friend of the Pines," was from Nagasaki, which was in those days the only port in Japan open to foreign trade. Yūshōshi is said to have been born of a liaison between a Chinese merchant and a local prostitute. When he went into business as a physician and was questioned about his background, Yūshōshi simply wrote that he was the son of a Nagasaki prostitute. People praised him for his honesty and strength of character.

According to records written by his students, Yūshōshi had no concern for reputation or profit, but he liked the good and despised the bad. Taking an interest in Buddhism and having a natural inclination for its teachings, his predilection was to heal people and save lives. For this purpose he studied both Taoist medical arts and Buddhist psychological arts from Chinese practitioners, and then meditated day and night for three years until he reached understanding.

Yūshōshi provided medical treatment on demand, with

remarkable results. He made his debut in Kyoto before he was even thirty years old and was the honored guest of barons from all over the country. It is also said that he was lauded by the founder and elders of the Ōbaku sect, a Chinese Zen school newly transplanted to Japan.

Yūshōshi was also versed in divination, geomancy, and astrology. They say he taught these subjects to his students, in accordance with their capacities.

One of Yūshōshi's peculiarities was that he would say just what he thought in discussions with other physicians, whether they were friends or strangers. If he saw that they were wrong, he would explain why he thought so, addressing them directly without any hesitation. If he heard someone say something mistaken, he would openly argue. He himself said that he did this to help others. In any case, as a result some doctors considered him mad, others considered him straightforward. Some praised him, others slandered him.

Shame and Conscience

There was a certain merchant who was deeply impressed by the lofty virtue of the Zen monk Hakuin. He used to present the monk with gifts of money and goods from time to time.

As it happened, the daughter of the merchant had a love affair with a family servant, resulting in the birth of a child. When the irate merchant demanded an explanation, his daughter said she had been impregnated by the monk Hakuin.

The merchant was furious: "To think that I gave alms to an evil shavepate like that for ten years!" Picking the baby up in his arms, the merchant took it right over to Hakuin.

Laying it in the Zen master's lap, the merchant gave him a tongue-lashing and left in a huff.

Hakuin didn't argue. He began to take care of the baby as if it were his own. People who saw him also believed he had fathered the child.

One winter day, when Hakuin was out begging for alms from house to house in the falling snow, carrying the infant with him as he went, the merchant's daughter saw them and was filled with remorse. In tears, she went to her father and confessed the truth.

Mortified, the merchant was totally at a loss. He rushed over to throw himself to the ground at the feet of Zen master Hakuin, begging his forgiveness.

Hakuin simply smiled and said, "The child has another father?"

Zen in Action

Zen master Man-an wrote to a lay student of Zen, "If you want to quickly attain mastery of all truths and be independent in all events, there is nothing better than concentration in activity. That is why it is said that students of mysticism working on the Way should sit in the midst of the material world.

"The Third Patriarch of Zen said, 'If you want to head for the Way of Unity, do not be averse to the objects of the six senses.' This does not mean that you should indulge in the objects of the six senses; it means that you should keep right mindfulness continuous, neither grasping nor rejecting the objects of the six senses in the course of everyday life, like a duck going into the water without its feathers getting wet.

"If, in contrast, you despise the objects of the six senses and try to avoid them, you fall into escapist tendencies and never fulfill the Way of Buddhahood. If you clearly see the essence, then the objects of the six senses are themselves meditation, sensual desires are themselves the Way of Unity, and all things are manifestations of Reality. Entering into the great Zen stability undivided by movement and stillness, body and mind are both freed and eased."

Hidden Virtue, Manifest Reward

Zen master Hakuin used to tell a story of when he was a young student, traveling around to see Zen teachers and meditating on emptiness, by which Zen followers seek to clear their minds of subjective imaginings in preparation for perception of objective truth.

On one occasion Hakuin was traveling in the company of two other Buddhist monks. One of them asked Hakuin to carry his baggage for him, pleading weakness and fatigue from illness.

The young Hakuin readily assented, taking his mind off the extra load by plunging even more deeply into his contemplation of emptiness.

Observing Hakuin's youth and zeal, the other monk decided to take a load off his own shoulders as well. Claiming illness like the first, he asked Hakuin to carry his baggage too.

In the spirit of Buddhist service, Hakuin took up the third load and continued on his way, immersing himself in emptiness more intently than ever.

Eventually the three monks reached a point where they could go on only by boat, so they boarded a ferry at the nearest landing. Completely exhausted by now, Hakuin collapsed into a heap and fell sound asleep.

When he awoke, the young seeker was momentarily

disoriented. It appeared that they had just docked, but he had no memory of the trip.

Noticing a foul odor, he looked around and saw that everyone was green in the face and covered with vomit. And they were looking at him very strangely.

It turned out that the ferry boat had run into a squall in the course of its passage and had been tossed about so violently that everyone, including the boatman himself, had become uncontrollably seasick.

Only the young Zen student Hakuin, so exhausted from carrying the baggage of his two companions that he slept right through the storm, had not been affected at all.

This, related Zen master Hakuin, was how he had first realized through his own experience that the principle that hidden virtue is manifestly rewarded is actually true.

Emptying Hell

A samurai in the employ of the provincial barony came to call on Zen master Hakuin.

The master asked the samurai, "What have you done?"

The samurai said, "I have always liked to listen to Buddhist teaching. I have become infected with an illness because of this."

Hakuin asked, "What is your illness like?"

The samurai said, "I first met a Zen teacher and searched into the principle of the essence of mind. Then I met a Shingon Discipline teacher and studied the esoteric canon. Developing doubt and confusion about these two schools, while in the midst of visualization of the letter *A*, there suddenly arose in my mind images of hells. When I tried to stop them by means of the principle of the essence of mind, the two visions clashed, so my mind has become disturbed.

In sleep I have nightmares, and when awake, I only toil at conceptual thinking."

Hakuin clucked his tongue and said, "Do you know what it is that fears hell?"

The samurai said, "The view of emptiness! I have caught this illness."

Hakuin shouted at the samurai again and again, shouting him away, saying, "You little knave! A samurai is someone who is so loyal to his lord that he does not flee floods or fires, and he exposes his body to spears and swords without quivering or blinking an eye. How can you fear the view of emptiness? Right now, fall into each of those hells, and let's check them out!"

The samurai complained, "How can a teacher have people fall into an evil state?"

Hakuin laughed and said, "The hells I fall into are eighty-four thousand in number! Look—there's nowhere I don't fall!"

Finally seeing the master's point, the samurai was overjoyed.

Everyday Religion

One of the great barons of western Japan went to visit the Zen master Hakuin and ask for some instruction. As it happened, a villager had brought some millet cakes for the Zen master just at the same time. Hakuin immediately took the cakes and offered them to the baron.

Accustomed to rich food, the baron had never eaten millet. He could not bring himself to eat of the peasant woman's simple cakes.

Observing this, Hakuin scolded the baron, saying, "Force yourself to eat it; you will get to know the misery of the common folk. My teaching is nothing but this."

Social Relations

In late feudal Japan, consumption of goods was regulated by detailed laws, which differed according to one's social class. Now in Zen master Hakuin's area there was a wealthy merchant, very conservative, whose household rules forbade the servants to carry umbrellas. The consequence of this rule, however, was simply that his servants used to keep umbrellas at the houses of friends, then use them as necessary when going out.

One day it happened that a certain maid of that merchant's house took a new umbrella she had purchased and brought it to the Zen master Hakuin, hoping to have him write her name on it for her. When she got to the temple, an assistant agreed to take the umbrella and relay her request to the master. He also explained to Hakuin the situation in the merchant's household.

Having listened to all this, Hakuin picked up a brush and wrote on the paper umbrella, "Whether it rains or pours, I won't disobey my employer."

The maid was delighted. Being illiterate, she couldn't read what the master had written. She assumed it was her name, as she had requested.

Then one rainy day, the maid asked for some time off to run an errand. As she went on her way, holding her umbrella over her against the rain, she began to notice that people were snickering at her. Wondering what the matter was, at length she asked someone about it, only to learn what was really written on her umbrella.

Furious, the woman went to Hakuin demanding compensation for her umbrella. Instead, the Zen master invited her in and talked to her about how to work for an employer.

Then Hakuin went to see the merchant himself. "A servant is someone's child too, you know," he said to the rich man, who was so moved by the great master's compassion that he changed the rules of his house.

Night Rain

Before he went to live in the mountains, Zen master Ranryo traveled throughout the four quarters, making no distinction between court and countryside, city and village, not avoiding even wineshops and brothels.

When someone asked him why he acted in this way, the Zen master said, "My Way is right there, wherever I happen to be. There is no gap at all."

Later Ranryo went into the mountains, where he built a simple hut and lived a life of frugal austerity as he continued to work on Zen.

Especially fond of night rain, Ranryo would burn incense and sit up on rainy nights, even until dawn. The people of the mountain villages, not knowing his name, used to call him "the Night Rain Monk." This amused him, so he began to use Night Rain as a literary name.

Once a visitor asked Ranryo about the relative merits of Zen meditation and the Pure Land Buddhist practice of Buddha-remembrance, reciting the name of the Buddha of Infinite Light. Ranryo gave his answer in verse:

> *Zen meditation and Buddha Remembrance*
> *are like two mountains;*
> *Higher and lower potentials*
> *divide a single world.*
> *When they arrive, all alike*
> *see the moon atop the peak;*
> *Only pity those who have no faith*
> *and suffer over the climb.*

The Door of Compassion

Jimon was the daughter of a samurai. Her mother died when she was eleven years old, and her father passed away a few years later, when she was fifteen. When she turned eighteen, she shaved her head and became a nun.

Jimon was rich in kindness and compassion, doing whatever she could to help those in need. One winter night, during a severe snowstorm, two little beggar boys showed up at her door. They looked so cold to her that she immediately took off her outer robe and gave it to them.

On that occasion, she composed a poem, saying,

> *The plight of the desolate—*
> *how wretched these sleeves*
> *too narrow for shelter*
> *to keep them*
> *from spending the night outside.*

On another freezing night, a burglar entered her cottage looking for money or other valuables. Jimon got up calmly and said, "You poor thing! Imagine crossing the fields and mountains to come here on a cold night like this! Wait a minute, and I'll make you something warm!"

So saying, Jimon boiled some gruel for the burglar, seating him by the fireside. Then as he ate, she began to talk to him. "I've renounced the world," she said, "so I have nothing of value. But you can take whatever you want.

"There is something, however, that I want from you in exchange. I've been watching you, and it seems to me that you could make a decent living doing any sort of work or business you wished. And yet here you are in this wretched state, not only disgracing yourself but also disgracing your family. Isn't that a shame?

"I want you to change your attitude and give up burglary.

Take everything in my cottage and pawn it for money to start a suitable business. You'll be much so much easier in mind that way!"

Profoundly moved, the young burglar voiced his thanks and left without taking anything at all.

Formation of a School

For ten years after his enlightenment, Gessen served as the abbot of a well-known monastery. Finally he left the monastery and went to live in a hermitage where no one knew who he was.

Mixing in with villagers, Gessen used to teach the local children reading, writing, and arithmetic, gradually introducing them to Buddhist ideas in an indirect manner.

Eventually Zen seekers from all over the country came looking for him. Finally there was not a barn or a cowshed within miles of his hermitage but had been rented as lodgings by students and followers of the great Zen master Gessen.

Mind and Essence

Ishida Baigan was a founder of *Shingaku* Mind Studies, a lay movement inspired by Zen Buddhism. Up until the time he was fifty years old, it is said, displeasure used to show on Baigan's face whenever something offended him. After the age of fifty, however, he never evinced any sign of pleasure or displeasure. When he reached the age of sixty, he said, "Now I have attained ease."

Once someone asked him, "Are mind and essence different?"

Baigan replied, "Mind includes both essence and sense; it has movement and stillness, substance and function. Essence is the substance, which is tranquil; mind, which moves, is the function. Speaking of mind in terms of essence, it resembles essence in a way; the substance of mind is unminding until it is disturbed; essence is also unminding. Mind is the realm of energy, essence is the realm of noumenon. Just as the moon is reflected even in a tiny drop of dew, noumenon is inwardly present in all things, even though it is invisible."

Temper

Once a man came to Zen master Bankei and confessed that he had been born with a short temper, which he found unmanageable in spite of his attempts to control it.

The Zen master said, "What an interesting thing you were born with! Do you have a short temper right now? If so, show me, and I'll cure it for you."

The man said, "I don't have it right at this moment. It comes out unexpectedly, when something happens."

The Zen master said, "In that case, your short temper is not something innate in you."

Sitting Meditation

Someone asked the great master Bankei about sitting Zen. He replied, "Harmonization with the ineffable wisdom inherent in everyone before getting involved in thinking and conceptualization is called meditation; detachment from all external objects is called sitting. Just closing your eyes and sitting there is not what I call sitting meditation; only sitting meditation attuned to subtle knowledge is to be considered of value.

"All confusion is a matter of revolving in vicious circles of delusion because of using thoughts. When angry thoughts come out, you become a titan; craving makes you an animal; clinging to things makes you a hungry ghost. If you die without giving these up, you revolve in routines forever, taking on all sorts of forms, whirling in the flow of birth and death.

"If you detach from thoughts, there is no confusion, so there is no cause or effect. There being no cause or effect, there is no revolving in routines. As long as you entertain thoughts, when you cultivate good thoughts there are good causes and effects, and when you do wrong there are bad causes and effects. When you have detached from thought and tuned into subtle knowledge, there are no causes or effects of birth or death.

"When I speak this way, it seems like a vision of nothingness, but it is not so. The reason I say that this it not nothingness is that when I say so, each of you hears it. Even though you do not think of hearing, because the original knowledge innate in everyone is effectively aware, you can hear distinctly. When you touch fire or water, you know it is hot or cold; yet no one *learns* to feel heat or cool.

"This is working beyond thought, so even if there is no thought, it cannot be called nothingness. This inherent subtle knowledge comprehends everything without involvement in the dualistic ideas of being and nothingness, just as a clear mirror reflects the images of things distinctly. So what discursive thought is necessary for this?

"Discursive thought is there because there is confusion. When you arrive at nondiscursive knowledge, you perceive and distinguish things before discursive thought, so in the end there is no confusion. That is why nondiscursive knowledge is valued.

"For this reason, sitting meditation with unfabricated subtle knowledge is the highest practice."

The Way to the Way

Sōkai had been in the congregation of Zen master Daiyū for a year when he suddenly had an insight one night as he was getting up from his meditation. Going to the teacher, Sōkai presented his understanding.

Daiyū said, "You have gotten into the hall, but you have not yet entered the room."

Sōkai asked, "Why do you say that?"

Daiyū quoted a scriptural saying: " 'Don't dwell on anything, yet enliven the mind,' " and he asked Sōkai, "What does it mean to 'yet enliven the mind'?"

Sōkai replied, "When you look for the mind, it cannot be found."

Daiyū said, "After all you haven't attained penetration."

Sōkai retorted, "I do not agree to doubt."

Raising his voice, Daiyū said, "No, no! If you really want to attain the Way, you must die completely once; only then can you realize it!"

Liberation

Ōhashi the courtesan was the daughter of a vassal of the shogun. She was sold into prostitution by her father after he had lost his position and been reduced to extreme poverty.

Ōhashi was charming, intelligent, and well educated in literature and the arts. As a result of her accomplishments, she became a famous courtesan in the red-light district of Kyoto.

Unable to reconcile herself to the misfortune that had befallen her, Ōhashi lapsed into an incurable depression and began to waste away.

One day a visitor noticed her condition and asked her if

she was depressed about something. Ōhashi explained to him how everything had come about. The visitor said, "No wonder you're sick! It would cost a thousand pieces of pure gold to cure your ailment! There is, nevertheless, a way to get free from it, but I'm afraid you won't believe."

Ōhashi insisted, "If you tell me the truth, how could I doubt? Please teach me!"

So the visitor explained to Ōhashi, "In your whole body, there is nothing that acts apart from perception and cognition. Perception and cognition have a host. Whatever you are doing, even when in a rush, look for this host within. What is it that sees? What is it that hears? If you practice this introspection earnestly and do not give up, your inherent Buddha-nature will suddenly appear. When you reach this state, you find it to be a shortcut to escape from the realm of misery."

Taking these words to heart, Ōhashi began to practice this introspective exercise in secret. Eventually she reached the point where there was no interruption in her inward attention.

Then one night a terrific thunderstorm arose, so violent that lightning struck in more than twenty places. Having always been terrified of thunder and lightning, Ōhashi huddled under her bedding with her servant girl.

Suddenly Ōhashi remembered the Zen exercise. Casting aside her fears, she sat bolt upright.

All at once a thunderbolt struck the courtyard. The impact threw Ōhashi flat on her back, knocking the wind out of her.

When she recovered her breath, Ōhashi noticed her perceptions were somehow different than usual, and she felt an indescribable joy.

Subsequently Ōhashi was released from bondage in the brothel when a man paid her debt and married her. She then sought out the Zen master Hakuin and spent the balance of her life deepening her understanding.

An Awakening

Zeshin spent many years living in seclusion on Mount Yoshino, outside the ancient capital city of Kyoto. There he practiced simply sitting, until one day his mind opened up and he forgot all his intellectual knowledge.

In a nearby temple there lived an old adept of the Sōtō school of Zen. Zeshin went to him and told him of his realization, seeking witness to his enlightenment. The adept said, "Master Bankei is the enlightened guide of the age. Go to him to study."

So Zeshin proceeded directly to Jizō temple east of Kyoto, where he was told Bankei was staying. At that time, however, the great master was in seclusion and was not receiving any visitors. Nevertheless, Zeshin came to the temple every day and sat outside the gate all day, returning to the city at night. He did this for thirteen days in a row.

Finally the keeper of the inn where Zeshin was staying asked him what was going on. Zeshin told him the facts as they were. Trying to help out, the innkeeper directed him to master Dokushō of nearby Saga.

Now Zeshin went to call on Dokushō and told him of his understanding. Dokushō simply said, "Keep it well." Zeshin left the same day and went back to Mount Yoshino.

Several months later, Zeshin set out again to try to see Bankei, the master of the age. On the way to Jizō temple, he heard that Bankei was then in Edo, the capital of the shoguns, where Bankei taught at Kōrin temple.

When Zeshin finally arrived, Bankei met with him right away.

When Zeshin had presented his understanding, Bankei said, "And the ultimate end?"

Zeshin hesitated, trying to think of something to say; then he hung his head.

This happened three times.

Finally Zeshin asked, "Is there an ultimate end?"

Zen master Bankei said, "You don't know how to use it."

Zeshin again hung his head, unable to say anything.

Something like this happened three times before Zeshin finally asked, "How is it used?"

At that moment, an oriole called out in the yard. Bankei said, "You hear the oriole when it cries."

Zeshin went into ecstasy. He prostrated himself before the Zen master three times.

Bankei said, "After this, don't speak vainly."

At the end of the summer meditation retreat at Kōrin temple, Bankei returned to his principal teaching center in western Japan. Zeshin followed him there.

For several days after his return, the Zen master met with newcomers. Each day Zeshin came before the Zen master with other new arrivals, but Bankei paid him no attention. This happened on three successive days, with Zeshin showing up to be seen by the master and Bankei saying nothing to him.

When the crowd had finally dispersed, at last Bankei addressed Zeshin, saying, "You're lucky. If you hadn't met me, you'd have become a braggart."

Still Alive

Kōsen studied Zen with master Ryōten, trying to meditate on emptiness. Ryōten admonished him, "Intensive Zen meditation must be like a mute having a dream. You are too intellectual to study Zen."

Far from being discouraged by this, Kōsen stirred himself to make even greater efforts. One night as he sat watching the rain, a boy monk called to him in a loud voice. Kōsen responded, then all of a sudden experienced an awakening of insight.

Later Kōsen went to study with Zen master Hakujun. One day the master quoted a famous line of scripture that says, "Don't dwell on anything, yet enliven the mind." Then he asked Kōsen, "What is 'the mind'?"

Kōsen said, "Not dwelling on anything!!!"

Hakujun punched him six or seven times and said, "You ignoramus! You still don't know the meaning of the words 'yet enliven,' do you?"

At that moment, Kōsen attained liberation.

Useless Suffering and Disbelief

Once Zen master Bankei said to a group of people, "When I was first inspired to seek enlightenment, because I did not find an enlightened teacher I practiced all sorts of austerities, wasting my body away.

"Sometimes I would cut off all human contact and live in isolation. Sometimes I would fashion a paper enclosure and sit inside it, or I would set up screens and sit in a dark room, sitting in the lotus position without lying down, until my thighs became ulcerated and festered, leaving permanent scars.

"Then when I'd hear of the existence of a teacher at such-and-such a place in such-and-such a province, I'd go there directly to meet him. After several years of this, there were few places in all of Japan that my footsteps had not reached.

"All this was due to the fact that I hadn't met an enlightened teacher. After my mind opened up one day, for the first time I realized how useless my years of toil and pain had been, and I attained peace.

"Now I tell you all how to attain fulfillment in your present lives without straining yourselves, but you don't completely believe in it. This is because you are not really serious."

Confessions of a Zen Master

Yui-e, an elder of the Sōtō school of Zen, came to Zen master Bankei and said, "I was inspired when I was seventeen or eighteen years old. For over thirty years I sat for long periods without lying down, concentrating single-mindedly, but found errant thoughts and false consciousness hard to erase. In recent years my mind and intellect have both become clear, and I have attained peace. How did you concentrate in the past?"

Bankei replied, "I too toiled over the occurrence of thoughts when I was young, but suddenly I realized that our school is the school of the enlightened eye, and no one can help another without clear perception. From the beginning I transcended all other concerns and concentrated on working solely on attainment of clear vision. For this reason, I have mastered the ability to see whether other people have true perception."

Mind and Mount

Once Zen master Bankei spent several nights sitting under a crucifix in an execution ground, testing his Zen mind. After that he lay down on an embankment surrounding a corral.

Now it so happened that there was a warrior in the corral

beating a horse. Seeing this, Bankei hollered, "Hey! What do you think you're doing?"

The warrior heard the Zen master shouting but paid no attention. Whipping his horse, he galloped past Bankei. Again the master shouted, "Hey! What do you think you're doing?"

This happened three times before the warrior stopped and got off his horse. Approaching the Zen master, he now saw that Bankei was not an ordinary man. The warrior said, "You were yelling at me. Do you have something to tell me?"

Bankei said, "Rather than beat your horse for being unruly, why not chastise yourself and train your own mind right?"

A Martinet

Enzui was a rare master. He never showed any sign of anger on his face and rarely even spoke. He never lay down to sleep and hardly ever ate. Neither material nor sexual desires ever occurred to him in his life.

One day Enzui's Zen teacher Manzan called him and gave him a scolding, saying, "Fasting and never lying down are inhibiting your potential for the Way. Diligence and meditation are decreasing your life of wisdom. Why not let go entirely, naturally going along with the flow, becoming a clean and free individual without contrivance or compulsion?"

Bowing in gratitude, Enzui left, covering his tears. After that he exerted himself even more, increasing his ascetic practices. One day his mind opened up, and he attained a state where there is no doubt.

Later on in life, Enzui returned to his native province and built a cloister there, vowing thenceforth never to go out into human society. Even if old acquaintances wrote to him, he didn't reply, and when Zen seekers knocked at his door, he didn't open up.

Enzui died in 1736, at the age of seventy. One of his followers related, "The teacher fasted and never lay down all his life, continuing these austerities even until the moment of his death, when he put on a formal robe and passed away sitting in a chair. Even after he died, his body remained upright, his posture of meditation still composed."

The Seed of Zen Practice

One day Zen master Shōsan said of a certain individual, "So-and-so is a great practitioner, is he not? He says that no matter what kind of plague he may die from, he wants to die as calmly as if he were taking a walk in the neighborhood."

One of the students in the group said, "He just thinks that way—he's not the kind of man to do Zen practice."

The master said, "Even if that is so, still he is a man with the seed of great Zen practice."

Last Words

When Tenkei was on his deathbed, he was surrounded by his congregation of disciples, who were weeping and wailing. The Zen master looked around at them and said, "When the Buddha was about to enter extinction, he was surrounded by monks, nuns, laymen, and laywomen, all crying in distress. The Buddha scolded them, saying, 'If you really understood the four holy truths, why would you weep?' I do not censure your weeping and wailing today, because you are not rid of attachment to the Teaching.

"Do you wonder why I say this? All my life I have been

upholding Zen Buddhism and working wholeheartedly for people, but human feelings are arrogant, the influence of education is weak, and very few people have faith. Imagining how there will be no guides to bring out the true teaching in the future, unawares I weep.

"Everything is conditional and ultimately empty of inherent selfhood. This is easy to state but hard to understand clearly. I'm afraid you may misunderstand it; but when you do really understand it, you are heirs of Buddha's teaching, repaying the boon of the Buddha and Zen founders. Upholding this principle, work for the benefit of others, on and on.

"If people who are not present here should come seeking me in the future, then tell them I said this on my deathbed, weeping as I spoke."

The Decline and Revival of Zen

Hakuin, the great Zen master who revived the Rinzai sect in the eighteenth century, studied with many teachers. It was Shōjū Rōjin, however, who opened his eyes to the depth and breadth of real Zen.

Shōjū used to say, "This Zen school of ours declined in the Sung dynasty [960–1278] and died out in the Ming dynasty [1368–1644]. Although some of the residual efficacy was transmitted to Japan, it is as faint as stars in daytime. This state of affairs is truly lamentable."

Shōjū also said, "Everywhere nowadays there are only lifeless imitators studying signposts, 'Zen teachers' without liberated vision. Such people haven't even dreamed of what is transmitted by the enlightened."

Later on, after his own enlightenment, Hakuin would tell people, "When I heard old Shōjū's criticisms, I wondered why he was so indignant about the Zen centers of the time, what with the proliferation of monasteries and the emergence of famous teachers. Later, when I traveled around the Zen world and saw a number of 'masters,' I did not run into a single true master with great insight. Only then did I realize how the Way of old Shōjū was far superior to those of other Zen centers."

Independence

Once Zen master Tenkei was formally invited to become the teaching abbot of a certain monastery. He refused, saying, "Decadence has been increasing for a long time; since the basis of the teaching has been lost, how can anyone appear in the world as a teacher? Say no more about it."

The emissary bringing the invitation responded, "The congregation at the monastery only wants to borrow you for the sake of the Great Teaching. Who would say that is heterodox?" And he kept begging the Zen master so insistently that Tenkei finally assented.

The following year, however, Tenkei withdrew from the monastery on account of a certain incident. He said in a verse,

> *Coming was fine, going's fine too;*
> *flowing water, a floating cloud—an individual mendicant.*
> *Why be led by the nose by other people?*
> *Going along with circumstances, today I am leaping again.*

Last Words

"Old Lady O-San" attained enlightenment while studying with Zen master Tetsumon. Later, when the great master Hakuin came to her province, O-San went to see him.

To test the woman, Hakuin asked her about "the sound of one hand clapping."

O-San promptly uttered a verse:

> *Rather than listen*
> *to Hakuin's sound*
> *of one hand clapping,*
> *clap both hands*
> *and do business!*

When O-San was in her final illness, she was surrounded by her children, who sought some last words from her. She smiled and intoned a verse:

> *In this world*
> *where words do not remain at all,*
> *any more than the dew*
> *on the leaves,*
> *whatever should I say*
> *for posterity?*

Birth and Death

Goshū came to Zen master Yui-e and said, "I have been studying Zen for many years, but have not yet succeeded. Please give me some guidance."

Yui-e said, "There is no secret trick to Zen study. It's just a matter of freedom from birth and death."

Goshū asked, "How does one pass through birth and death to freedom?"

Raising his voice, Yui-e said, "Your every passing thought is birth and death!"

At these words Goshū went into ecstasy, feeling as if he had put down a heavy burden.

A Reformed Heretic

Ummon began to study Confucian books and religious texts when he was fourteen or fifteen years old. At the age of twenty-two, however, he had a change of heart. "Even if I read every exoteric and esoteric book in existence," he reflected, "what good will that do on the border of life and death?"

After that he gave away all of his books and abandoned academic studies.

Subsequently Ummon went to see a Zen master, who taught him to work on koans.

Ummon protested, "I don't want to work on koans. Just knowing for myself a state of total death and complete cessation, having become a pile of ashes, I do not entertain any doubts. In the course of daily activities, what is going on? Is it there? Is it not? As long as I ask myself this, that is enough."

The Zen master said, "If you act like that, you will become a heretic."

Ummon retorted, "Even if I become a heretic, it is enough to have attained peace of mind."

Ummon continued to meditate single-mindedly for another two years.

One day as he was gathering firewood in the forest, Ummon felt the whole world collapse, including himself. In that instant he attained cosmic joy.

After that Ummon reflected, "Although I have attained my own peace and happiness, this is no more than the principle of the standard canonical teachings. What about the Zen message that is specially transmitted outside of doctrine?"

So he redoubled his efforts for another two years, until

he finally discovered the living experience of Zen. Now his mind was completely released.

When Ummon was about to die, he admonished his students in these terms: "I have four statements. First is to cut through all mental entanglements, to rely on universal truth. Second is to let go of body and mind, to shed birth and death. Third is to transcend the absolute, to establish an individual life. Fourth is to haul rocks and carry earth, to perpetuate the life of wisdom."

Ummon's parting verse said,

> *The last word*
> *lights up the heavens*
> *and lights up the earth.*

An Eccentric Sage

Entsū was an eccentric sage of the little known Ōbaku school of Zen. An unconventional man, he went where he wanted and did what he wished. He lived alone, not staying in any fixed place. Hardly anything about his life is known for sure.

Once Entsū was in the city of Kyoto to pay a visit to a certain family. In the hubbub, the simpleminded Zen master forgot where he was going. Not knowing what else to do, he began knocking on doors, one after another, asking whoever answered, "Is this the house Entsū is supposed to visit?"

On another occasion, someone asked Entsū to write a preface for a certain book. Entsū agreed, but he scribbled so badly that the preface was illegible in many places. The man who had requested the writing brought it back to Entsū to ask him what it said.

The Zen master examined his own writing again and again, then finally declared, "I can't read it either! One of my students is good at reading my writing—you'd better show it to him."

Zen Scholarship

Honkō was an unusually talented Zen master, irrepressibly outstanding, with a wide learning and a powerful memory. His own Zen teacher Shigetsu had been one of the greatest scholarly masters. Honkō himself used to travel around lecturing on Zen at the invitation of centers all over the country.

Among Honkō's voluminous writings is a commentary on parts of the redoubtable *Shōbōgenzō,* which is the magnum opus of the great thirteenth-century Zen master Dōgen. The first and only great Buddhist work written in classical Japanese, *Shōbōgenzō* is one of the most difficult works in the canon.

While Honkō was working on his commentary on *Shōbōgenzō,* a monk involved in the study of logic came to him requesting that he expound the *Śūrangama-sūtra,* a most abstruse and complex work in the Chinese language.

At once the Zen master placed the *Śūrangama-sūtra* on the left side of the desk, set the *Shōbōgenzō* on the right, and put a piece of paper in the middle. Then he proceeded to lecture on the *Śūrangama-sūtra* while simultaneously reading the *Shōbōgenzō* and writing a commentary on it, keeping his attention on all three tasks without confusion.

Those who observed this were astounded, and rumors began to circulate that Honkō was an incarnation of a spirit or a saint.

Long Journey Home

Daikyū's exceptional nature was evident even when he was still just a child. Teachers of all schools of Buddhism sought to enroll him as a disciple, but his parents refused to give their permission.

Nevertheless, Daikyū finally left home to enter Zen discipleship when he was only five years old.

When Daikyū was in his fifteenth year, one day he happened to hear his teacher talking to someone about something he called "the state before birth." This made Daikyū wonder, and he used to sit and meditate whenever he had any free time.

Later on, Daikyū went to see Zen master Zōkai in Kyoto, to ask about the essentials of concentration. On the way there, he kept his attention on the tip of his nose, so he didn't even see the clamor and fanfare of the ancient capital even as he walked through it. So absorbed was he in concentration that he bumped into numerous horse carriages on the road, their drivers hollering at him as he continued unminding on his way.

Having met the master Zōkai, Daikyū asked permission to remain there to study Zen. Zōkai assented and gave Daikyū the task of attending to the master's medicine. Daikyū was eighteen years old at that time.

One day when Daikyū went to throw away some herbal waste, he forgot himself completely on reaching the river. Even though it was the season when the maples turn scarlet as brocade, he didn't even see them. Such was the pinpoint intensity of his concentration. People used to call him "the Entranced Attendant."

At the age of twenty-three, Daikyū went to meet the famous Zen master Kogetsu and expressed his perception to him. Kogetsu said, "Your perception is after all that of an outsider. It would be completely useless on the shore of life and death. Focus your mental energy intensely, and someday you will naturally attain unification."

Then Kogetsu taught Daikyū a set of twelve poems by an ancient Chinese Zen master and had him use these to guide him in his daily and nightly meditations.

One day the next summer, as Daikyū was carrying a tea bottle to the storehouse, he suddenly felt as if he were walking in space, his mind solid as iron. As he stopped and stood there, a clear wind blew into his chest. Continuing on his way, he bumped into a pillar and suddenly had an insight.

Daikyū went to Zen master Kogetsu and said, "Today I have finally gotten through the obstruction in my heart!"

Kogetsu just smiled.

After several years of further study with Kogetsu, Daikyū thought he had mastered Zen completely. Figuring there was no one anywhere who could teach him anything anymore, Daikyū decided to seek out a place of retreat to mature his realization.

In the course of his journey, however, Daikyū happened to read a verse written by the great Zen master Hakuin. It was so extraordinary that Daikyū determined to go see Hakuin in person.

When Daikyū met Hakuin, he found the great master a truly impressive Zen personality. Daikyū soon asked permission to continue his Zen studies with Hakuin.

Already a longtime seeker, Daikyū had a notebook in which he had recorded every Zen statement he had mastered. Determined to make a fresh start in Hakuin's tutelage, he now took his precious notebook and burned it.

Daikyū was twenty-six years old at this time.

One day, Daikyū accompanied Hakuin on a visit to Unzan, another Zen master. In the course of conversation, the subject of the Zen classic *The Blue Cliff Record* came up. Unzan asked Hakuin which verse in that collection he considered best. Hakuin named a certain verse, and Unzan agreed.

Daikyū, who was sitting there listening to the conversation of the two elder masters, was thoroughly bewildered by what he heard. He himself had been studying Zen for more than twenty years, and yet he was unable to make such fine distinctions as the elder masters.

On their way back, Daikyū wanted to tell Hakuin what he had realized, but he found it hard to convey. Following the great master along the road, Daikyū stepped forward several times, trying to get Hakuin to stop and talk to him.

Aware that Daikyū was ripe for a breakthrough, Hakuin deliberately brushed him off and kept on going.

Thoroughly upset, Daikyū went to sit on the veranda of a house by the roadside.

After meditating for a good while, Daikyū suddenly had an insight. Opening his eyes, he found that Hakuin was long gone.

Running back to the temple, Daikyū presented his understanding to Hakuin. The elder master attested to the truth of his realization.

Not long after that, Daikyū left Hakuin. As he was parting, he asked the great master, "What is the primary formula?"

Hakuin said, "A, B, C."

Daikyū asked, "What is the secondary formula?"

Hakuin said, "M, N, O."

Daikyū bowed and departed.

Hakuin's assistant, Zen master Tōrei, overheard this exchange. Later on he said to his followers, "That Daikyū is really crude; he didn't even ask about the tertiary formula. I hope he comes here sometime, so I can poke into the matter for him."

When Daikyū was twenty-nine years old, he went back to look after his first teacher, who was now a very old man. One night Daikyū sat until very late, when he happened to hear a dog howl. At that moment his mind suddenly opened up, and he attained great enlightenment, shedding his previous knowledge and views all at once.

The next day he went to see Seizan, a Zen master he had worked with in the past. Before Daikyū had said a word, Seizan said to him, "I knew you had potential for enlightenment from the very start. I have been waiting here for a long time for you to catalyze it on your own. It seems to be a matter of timing. I conceal nothing from you; now I have bequeathed to you the treasury of the eye of truth."

Daikyū simply bowed.

Eventually Daikyū became a Zen teacher. He was very strict. "Once universal life is manifest," he would demand of his students, "why can't you pass through to freedom?" To his profound regret, no one in his congregation realized what he meant.

In the spring of his fifty-ninth year, Daikyū fell ill. Realizing his end was near, he presented his spiritual heir with tokens of successorship, including the robe of the faith representing transmission of Buddhist precepts and a document of the precise lineage of masters.

When Daikyū's condition became critical, followers surrounding him asked for a final statement.

Drawing himself up majestically, Daikyū assumed a joyful appearance. With a smile he opened his eyes, making sure everyone saw him do this. Then he passed away sitting there in a state of serene calm.

A Drunken Buddha

Suiwō and Tōrei were Zen master Hakuin's two most capable assistants. Suiwō was known as a master of great capacity, Tōrei as a master of subtle detail. Many of Hakuin's later successors actually received their advanced training from one or both of these younger masters.

Suiwō was already over thirty years old when he met Hakuin for the first time. Nothing whatsoever is known of his early life. The great master Hakuin saw Suiwō to be a man of exceptional spirit, and pressed him very hard to realize his potential.

Suiwō spent twenty years in Hakuin's school, but he lived ten miles away and never came to the temple except when there was a lecture. His private consultations with the teachers always took place late at night, so no one ever saw Suiwō coming or going. On lecture days he would leave as soon as the talk was over. Thus it was hardly realized that Suiwō was Hakuin's disciple.

Suiwō was eccentric by nature. Fond of rice wine, he paid no attention to trivial matters, and often spoke and acted outside the bounds of normal convention. He hardly sat in meditation at all and scarcely read any scripture. He had no fixed abode but would sprawl out to sleep wherever he might be, considering himself lucky if he had managed to obtain enough wine to get tipsy. He enjoyed hobbies of chess and painting and lived life as he pleased. People couldn't decide whether he had hidden depths or was just a shallow man.

Although Suiwō did not care to live in Hakuin's temple, when the great master was in his final illness, Suiwō came back to take care of him. After Hakuin died, Suiwō inherited the temple, but he didn't do anything. Whenever people came to study Zen, Suiwō would simply tell them to go to

Tōrei. Yet in spite of his refusal to talk about Zen, there were never fewer than seventy or eighty seekers surrounding him.

Now Daikyū and Reigen, Zen masters who had also studied with Hakuin, began writing letters to Suiwō urging him to get to work. In spite of their efforts, however, Suiwō remained serenely unmoved.

Seven years after Hakuin's passing, Daikyū, Reigen, and Tōrei finally converged on Suiwō and insisted that he be the master of ceremonies for the traditional seven-year memorial service to be held for Hakuin by his disciples. Unable to refuse, Suiwō rose to the occasion by lecturing on the Five Houses of Zen to an assembly of more than two hundred.

Suiwō was about fifty-eight years old at this time. Now the ranks of his followers swelled to more than a hundred. They lived in individual quarters all over the area, and there was not enough time for Suiwō to meet with them all when they came to see him.

Suiwō was also invited to speak at other places, attracting audiences of three to five hundred. In later years he drew as many as seven and eight hundred listeners to his lectures on the Zen classics.

Suiwō used to tell people, "An ancient said that it is preferable to be too relaxed than too intense. I do not agree; it is better to be too intense than too relaxed." He would add, "Don't be weak and dependent. Someone who keeps on seeking the truth unremittingly can penetrate in one or two nights."

Suiwō also used to say, "Everywhere else they are orderly and regular, their ceremonious bearing models of dignity. Here we have elephant eyes and monkey noses, with no hair on the shins. Of what use are worldlings making a living by reciting scriptures?"

Speaking of the school of his old teacher Hakuin, Suiwō said, "The only one of his followers who snatched all the spiritual goods from Hakuin's house was Tōrei. The only one who penetrated deeply into the source of his teaching was Daikyū."

Suiwō also said, "Even Zen monks who traveled freely throughout the land without inhibition found themselves at a loss when they met Hakuin. Why was this? Because 'brambles reached the sky, barbed wired covered the ground,' so that they could neither advance nor retreat. Therefore they had their flags and drums taken away, so they took off their armor and surrendered. None of the other Zen congregations have these brambles; that is why monks stride right past them, and they are unable to trip up anyone at all. I guess that's fitting."

When Suiwō was on his deathbed, his attendants asked for a parting verse. Suiwō scolded them. When they repeated the request, he took a brush and wrote,

> *I've been fooling*
> *Buddhas and Zen masters*
> *for seventy-three years.*
> *As for the final statement,*
> *What? What?*
> *Kaaa!*

Closing his eyes, he passed away.

The Master of Subtle Detail

Tōrei first studied Zen with master Kogetsu. Later on he went through a severe apprenticeship with Hakuin.

Well prepared by his work with Kogetsu, Tōrei soon attained awakening under Hakuin's tutelage. Within a few years, he had learned the whole of Hakuin's inner teaching.

Unfortunately, the duress of Tōrei's exertions broke his body down, and he fell mortally ill. Finding no medical treatment of any avail, Tōrei thought to himself, "Even though I have found out all about the source and the methods of Zen, what good will that do if I should suddenly die?"

So he wrote a book called *The Inexhaustible Lamp of Zen*. Showing it to Hakuin, he said, "If there is anything worthwhile in this book, I'd like to pass it on to future generations. If it's a bunch of claptrap, however, I'll toss it right in the fire."

Hakuin took a look at it and said, "This will be medicine to open the eyes of later generations."

Then Tōrei left Hakuin and went to Kyoto, where he lived quietly, taking care of his illness, resigned to accept whatever was in store for him, death or life.

One day while he was in a mindless state, all at once Tōrei saw through Hakuin's lifetime experience. From that point on he recovered spontaneously.

Overcome with joyfulness, Tōrei wrote Hakuin a letter, telling him what had happened. The great master called Tōrei back and made him his Zen successor.

After Tōrei's recovery, he and Hakuin collaborated to set up a curriculum for a Zen school. Most of the work on the detailed examinations in the curriculum was evidently done by Tōrei. Late in Hakuin's life, when his energy finally waned, Tōrei worked hard to prod and encourage the disciples. Many of Hakuin's last disciples were crude in their realization; the outstanding ones were those whose fine tuning was completed by Tōrei.

Buddhahood in This Life

Once Zen master Tōrei was giving a talk on the Teaching in Saga, on the mountainous outskirts of Kyoto. It was the dead of winter, and the weather was so cold that everyone in the audience looked intensely uncomfortable.

Tōrei bellowed, "Those of you who are cowed by cold weather should return to mundane life right away! How can you learn Zen? Why don't you look for it in your own hearts? Fish are in the midst of water, yet do not know the water is there; people are in the midst of sublime truth, but do not know the truth."

In the audience at that time was an early follower of the Mind Studies movement, a man named Nakazawa Dōni, who was later to establish Mind Studies in eastern Japan. Hearing these words from Zen master Tōrei, he suddenly attained enlightenment. "Exposition of the Teaching means not putting the mind on externals," he later explained, adding, "This is what they mean by attaining Buddhahood in this very body."

Premature Recognition

Ryōzai first studied Zen with Kogetsu. Later he followed Hakuin, under whose tutelage he attained awakening.

When Ryōzai came to Hakuin, the great teacher saw at once that he had an unusual capacity. Ryōzai spent several years with Hakuin, eventually receiving his recognition as a Zen master. Thus Ryōzai became the first of many teachers to be trained by the great Zen master Hakuin.

Later on, however, Hakuin would say to people, "I gave Ryōzai the seal of approval too soon. Because of this, he cannot master things now. If I had waited another three years before giving him permission to teach, no one in the world would be able to criticize him."

Someone asked Hakuin why he had given Ryōzai approval so soon. The great master said, with deep regret,

"At that time, I was only conscious of how difficult it is to find such an individual. I didn't realize it was too soon."

The Great Work

Gasan went traveling when he was only sixteen years old. Entering a Zen cloister, in ninety days of intense work he attained some insight. After that, he went from teacher to teacher, studying with more than thirty Zen masters. None of them could do anything for him, so he returned to his original teacher Gessen.

Gessen recognized young Gasan's mastery and suggested that he give up wandering. At that time, Gasan himself also believed that he had mastered Zen.

Now it happened that Gasan had passed by Zen master Hakuin's school from time to time, but he had no desire to meet the famous teacher.

One day, however, he reflected, "Of the many teachers all over the land I have seen, not one could point out anything to me. Hakuin is the only one whose methods I do not know."

This thought inspired in Gasan the desire to meet Hakuin. He told Gessen of his intention. Gessen said, "Why should you necessarily meet Hakuin?" Gasan again thought he was right and stayed where he was.

Another year passed, when Gasan happened to hear that Hakuin had been invited to lecture on the classic *The Blue Cliff Record* in Edo, the capital city. Now he thought, "As long as I haven't seen that old teacher, I am not really a great man."

Even though Gessen tried to stop him again, now Gasan was determined to go. He traveled straight to Edo to meet the great master Hakuin.

When Gasan had presented his understanding, Hakuin

hollered, "What charlatan have you come from to foul me with so much bad breath?" And he tossed Gasan out.

But Gasan didn't give up. After being thrown out three times, he still thought he was really enlightened and that Hakuin was just trying to break him down on purpose.

Then one night as the lecture series was about to end, Gasan reflected, "It is in fact true that Hakuin is the greatest teacher in the land. Why would he reject people arbitrarily? He must have a point."

Now Gasan went to apologize to Hakuin for being rude, and asked for some instruction. Hakuin said, "You are immature. You'll pass your whole lifetime carrying a belly-skin of Zen around. Even if you can speak glibly, that won't empower you when you reach the shore of life and death. If you want to make your everyday life intensely satisfying, you must hear the sound of one hand clapping."

Later Gasan said to his own disciples, "I spent almost twenty years traveling all over the country, studying with more than thirty teachers. I was so sharp that none of them could cope with me. Finally I ran into old Hakuin and was kicked out three times, finding my usual empowerment useless at this point. Then I became a sincere follower.

"At that time, who in the world could have hit me but Hakuin? I do not value the greatness of his virtue or the breadth of his fame. I do not value the transcendence of his perception or his clear and thoroughgoing insight into the complex koans of the ancients. I do not value his fluent explanations or his fearless expositions. I do not value the number of his followers. I only value the fact that whereas all the other Zen teachers in the land could do nothing with me, by means of his harsh measures Hakuin managed to bring me to an impasse, finally enabling me to finish the Great Work.

"Obviously, this work is not at all easy. I followed

Hakuin for only four years, when he was so old that he was sometimes too tired for interviews. As a result, I called on master Tōrei and learned the highest teachings from him. If Tōrei hadn't been there, I would never have been able to work out the last details."

Stern Measures

Izu studied Zen with Hakuin for a long time. As a teacher in his own right, Izu inherited the harsh manner of the redoubtable master Hakuin but was even sterner. Whenever he would receive people asking about Zen, he would lay a naked sword next to his seat. If they were hesitant or argumentative, he would chase them out with the sword.

Learning How to Learn

Teishū was unusually sharp by nature, and his erudition embraced both religious and secular classics. The only thing he could not understand was the principle of the *I Ching,* the ancient *Book of Change.*

Wishing to complete his learning, Teishū set out for the capital city of Edo to question the elder Confucian scholars about *The Book of Change.* Along the way, he passed by the temple of Zen master Hakuin. Since Hakuin was known as one of the greatest masters in the land, Teishu decided to seek lodging there and see him.

When they met, Hakuin asked, "Where are you going?" Teishū said, "To Edo." Hakuin asked, "What for?" Teishū said, "I don't understand the principle of *The Book of Change,* so I want to listen to the lectures of the elder scholars in the capital."

Hakuin said, *"The Book of Change* can hardly be understood without the power of seeing the essence of mind.

Why don't you stay here for a while and try to see your essence? If you perceive the essence of mind, I will expound *The Book of Change* for you."

Teishū replied, "I will do just as you say." And he stayed there with Hakuin for intensive work. When the time was ripe, he forgot his doubts and actually did awaken.

A Mistake

Chōdō studied Zen with master Kogetsu and realized the state of Nothingness.

Now at this time, the school of Zen master Hakuin was flourishing, and seekers from all over the country were flocking to the great teacher.

Chōdō wanted to go and have a Zen debate with Hakuin, but Kogetsu advised him not to go. Chōdō wouldn't listen, so Kogetsu said, "If you insist, then let me write a letter of introduction."

So Chōdō headed for Hakuin's place, carrying a letter of introduction from Kogetsu.

Chōdō reached the temple where Hakuin lived just as the great master was taking a bath. Barging right in, Chōdō presented his understanding. Hakuin said, "If you are this way, you haven't come here for naught. But go take a rest for now."

Now Chōdō thought that Hakuin also approved of him.

When Hakuin at length emerged from the bath, Chōdō went to meet with him formally, presenting the letter of introduction from Kogetsu.

Opening the letter from Chōdō's teacher, Hakuin found that it simply said, "This youngster is not without some insight, but he is a man of small measure. Please deal with him expediently." Hakuin immediately hollered at Chōdō, "You have a small capacity and an inferior potential. What good will it do to consider this completion of the Great Work?"

Having his view snatched away, Chōdō immediately went mad and never recovered. He went back to his hometown and built a little meditation hall, where he practiced Zen discipline by himself.

In Zen monasteries it is traditional to observe a special session of intensive meditation in the first week of the last month of the year commemorating the enlightenment of the Buddha. Chōdō used to bring child monks and cats to his meditation hall on these occasions and have them sit. When the cats would run away, Chōdō would catch them and beat them for breaking the rules.

Hakuin used to lament, "I have taught many people, but I only made mistakes in two cases, that of Chōdō and one other."

Talking and Listening

Gettan used to say to his companions, "When you have a talking mouth, you have no listening ears. When you have listening ears, you have no talking mouth. Think about this carefully."

The Eleventh Hour

Chōsha used to come to participate in the special annual intensive meditation session with Zen master Hakuin every single year, yet he never attained anything.

Finally one year Hakuin said to him at the conclusion of the session, "You come here every year, just like a duck diving into the water when it is cold. You are making a long journey in vain, without gaining half a bit of empowerment. I can't imagine how many straw sandals you have worn out over the years making this trip. I have no use for idlers like you around here, so don't come anymore!"

Deeply stirred, Chōsha thought to himself, "Am I not a man? If I do not penetrate through to realization this time, I will never return home alive. I will concentrate on meditation until I die."

Setting himself a limit of seven days, Chōsha went to sit in a fishnet shed by the seashore.

But even after seven days of sitting in meditation without eating or sleeping, Chōsha was still at a loss. There was nothing for him to do but drown himself in the ocean.

Removing his shoes in the traditional manner of a suicide rite, Chōsha stood in the waves. At that moment, seeing the shimmering ocean and the rising sun merging into a crimson radiance, all at once he became completely empty and greatly awakened.

The Stone Robe

Nobody knows the real name of the Zen master they called the Stone Robe Monk. He lived alone in the neighborhood of Hakuin's temple and used to call on the great teacher from time to time.

A solitary individual, the master was so poor that he did not even own a robe. On very cold nights, he used to walk around his hut carrying a rock until he warmed up. Thus the local people took to calling him the Stone Robe Monk.

Later he disappeared. No one knows where he died, but the rock he used to carry around still sits in front of the hut.

Something from Nothing

Once on a journey Zen master Zenkō happened to see a ruined temple that he thought should be restored.

Completely without material resources of his own, Zenkō wrote a large sign saying, "This month, on such-and-such a day, the pilgrim Zen master Zenkō will perform a self-cremation. Let those who will donate money for firewood come watch."

Now Zenkō posted this sign here and there. Soon the local people were agog, and donations began pouring in.

On the appointed day, people jammed the temple, awaiting the lighting of the fire. Zenkō sat in the firewood, preparing to immolate himself. He called for the fuel to be ignited at his signal.

Now Zenkō went into silent meditation. A long time passed. All of a sudden, he looked up at the sky and nodded. Then he addressed the crowd, saying, "Listen, listen! There are voices in the clouds! Just as I was about to enter into extinction, the saints all said, 'It is still too early for you to think of leaving the defiled world! Put up with this world for a while, and stay here to save living beings.' So I can't go on with the cremation today."

Then he took the money that had been donated and was able to restore the abandoned temple with it.

Buddhism and the World

When Satsume was sixteen years old, she thought to herself, "Although I am not very beautiful, fortunately my body is sound. Undoubtedly I am to be married soon; I hope I get a handsome man."

Now she began to visit a certain shrine to pray, and she also started reciting a special scripture day and night. Even while she was doing her sewing and washing, the words of the scripture were constantly on her lips.

After several days of continual recitation, Satsume suddenly experienced an awakening of insight.

On one occasion, her father looked into her room and saw her sitting grandly on top of a copy of a Buddhist scripture. He was alarmed, thinking she may have gone mad; he gently admonished her, "What do you mean by sitting on a precious scripture? You will surely be punished by the Truth."

Satsume replied, "How is the wonderful scripture any different from my backside?"

Now her father thought this was even more bizarre; he went to tell the Zen master Hakuin.

Hakuin said, "I have a method that will help." He wrote a short poem, which he handed over and said, "Paste this on the wall of your home, where she will be sure to see it."

The poem said,

Hearing the call
of a silent raven
in the dark of night,
one misses one's father
before being born.

The man took the verse and did with it as Hakuin said. When she saw it, Satsume said, "This is the handwriting of master Hakuin. So even Hakuin only understands this much!"

Her father thought this was strange too, and told Hakuin about it. Hakuin said, "Bring Satsume here with you. I'll test her."

So Satsume and her father both came to visit Hakuin. The Zen master questioned the young woman closely, and Satsume answered fluently. Hakuin then presented a couple of koans. Satsume started thinking about them, but Hakuin said, "Go focus your mind on them."

Over a period of several days, Satsume passed through

several levels of koans. Hakuin finally taught her that which goes beyond, but Satsume resisted and would not accept it. The Zen master then threw her out.

Satsume was ejected several times like this. By the time half a year had passed, she had seen through that which goes beyond and had thoroughly studied the most intricate and puzzling stories of the ancients. She was now a Zen master, even though still in her teens.

At this point, Satsume's father began looking for a suitable husband for her. At first she refused and would not marry, but Hakuin called her to him and said, "You have already seen through enlightened reality, so why should you reject mundane reality? What is more, marriage is an important duty for men and women. It would be better for you to go along with your father." So it was that Satsume got married.

After Satsume's passing, Hakuin's successor Suiwō said to his own disciples, "When our former teacher was alive, there were very many laywomen with perfectly clear insight. There were those among them like Old Lady Satsu who were even beyond the reach of experienced Zen monks."

When Satsume was in her late years, she grieved exceptionally deeply over the loss of a granddaughter. The old man who lived next door chided her, "Why are you mourning so grievously? If people hear you, they'll wonder how you could still be acting like this even after having studied with Zen master Hakuin and attained insight into the essential. Please cut it down a little bit."

Satsume glared at the old man and retorted, "What do you know, baldy? My weeping and wailing are better for my granddaughter than incense, flowers, and lamps."

The Purely Mental Pure Land

Once a certain woman, whose name no one knows, attended a lecture by Hakuin. In his talk, the Zen master said, "The purely mental Pure Land, the Buddha in one's own being: once the Buddha appears, everything in the world radiates great light. If people want to perceive this, just turn to your own heart and seek single-mindedly.

"Since it is a purely mental Pure Land, how is the Pure Land arrayed? Since it is the Buddha in one's own being, what characteristics and refinements does the Buddha have?"

Hearing this, the woman thought, "That is not too hard." Returning home, she began to look into this day and night, bringing it to mind whether awake or asleep. Then one day, as she was washing a pot, she suddenly broke through.

Tossing aside the pot, she went to see Hakuin. She said, "I have come across the Buddha in my own body. Everything radiates with light. Marvelous! Marvelous!" She was so happy that she was dancing with joy.

Hakuin said, "This is what you say, but what about a cesspool? Does that radiate light?"

The woman went up and slapped Hakuin. "This old fellow isn't through yet," she said.

Hakuin roared with laughter.

The Dawn of Truth

Genrō traveled all over Japan visiting Zen masters from the time he was nineteen years old. Eventually he thought to himself, "The teachers everywhere are alike, giving guidance at random. They are unreliable. If I remain in a community, I will waste a lot of time on trivial things. It would be better for me if I lived alone in a deserted place in order to meditate single-mindedly."

One afternoon as he watched the setting sun, Genrō sighed to himself, "I have already spent five years working on Zen day and night. If I just spend my days this way, when will I ever pass all the way through?"

Genrō then sat on a boulder and plunged into intense concentration. Without realizing it, he sat there all through the night. Unaware of the breaking of dawn, Genrō suddenly heard the bell of a distant temple. At that moment his mind opened up and he attained great enlightenment.

Twenty-four years old at the time, Genrō composed an extemporaneous verse on this happy occasion:

> At dawn, in response to the temple bell, the universe opens;
> The orb of the sun, bright, comes from the Great East.
> What this principle is, I do not know;
> Unawares my jowls are filled with gales of laughter.

What Kind of Warrior

Seisetsu was most extraordinary even as a child. He left home and became a monk when he was just a boy.

Once the baron of the province came to visit the master of the temple on his way to the capital city. After they had chatted awhile, the master called little Seisetsu and had him pound the baron's back for him, to relieve the fatigue of the journey. The baron promised the boy that he would bring a religious robe for him on the way back from the capital the next year.

When the baron's stay in the capital city was over, he stopped by to see the Zen master again on his way back to his home fortress. The master had Seisetsu pound the baron's back for him this time as well, and the boy asked about the robe.

"I completely forgot," said the baron.

"What kind of samurai is this," exclaimed the boy, "who says one thing and does another?" Then he gave the baron a clout on the head and walked out.

The baron was deeply impressed by the unusual capacity of the boy, and he told the Zen master to take good care of him.

Later on Seisetsu studied with Gessen and Gasan, and went on to become one of the most redoubtable Zen teachers in the land.

Once when Seisetsu was seeing to the rebuilding of part of the monastery where he was teaching, a certain wealthy merchant came with a hundred ounces of gold, saying he wanted to donate it for the reconstruction project. Seisetsu took it without a word.

The next day the merchant came back to visit the Zen master. He remarked, "Although what I gave you was not so great an amount, it was an exceedingly costly donation for me. In spite of that, you didn't say a word of thanks. Why is that?"

Seisetsu hollered, "I am planting your field of blessings; why should I thank you?"

The merchant was very embarrassed. He apologized and thanked the Zen master.

Iron Face

Buttsū and Genrō were known throughout Japan as two of the fiercest Zen masters in the land. They were so ferocious in the ways they handled seekers that they were called Genrō the Wolf and Buttsū the Tiger.

Nobody knows where Buttsū came from or what his original name was. Some say he was originally a warrior from eastern Japan. He studied Zen for a long time and finally completed the Great Work. In his verse on awakening, he wrote,

> This matter's been on my mind for eighteen years;
> how many times have I gotten power
> yet still couldn't sleep at peace?
> One call, one answer, and clarity is complete:
> I've vomited out the bellyful of Zen
> that I had learned before.

Buttsū had a face of iron, severe and cold. He trained Zen students with harsh methods, not allowing human feelings to enter into the process at all. Many seekers who came to him could not bear this and left.

In the middle of the night of his death, Buttsū looked around and said, "Shall I go now?" Then he passed away while sitting in meditation, as though he had fallen asleep.

Penetrating Zen

When Inzan was nine years old, a certain Zen master saw him and immediately realized that he was not ordinary. The Zen master went to the boy's home and persuaded his parents to let him become a monk.

The parents were easily convinced. "He was never of this world," they said, as they gave their permission for the boy to leave home to enter a Zen Buddhist order.

When Inzan was sixteen years old, he left his temple to seek a teacher to guide him to ultimate enlightenment and liberation. First he followed Bankoku, who taught the unique method of the late great master Bankei to a large congregation of followers. Three years later he went to Gessen, who was noted for the harsh manner of his way of teaching.

When Inzan arrived at Gessen's place, he was informed

by the temple manager that there was no room for any more students. The manager suggested that Inzan was still rather young and would have time for intensive Zen practice later and that he might do well to go elsewhere to pursue academic studies in the meantime.

But Inzan was determined to study Zen with master Gessen. He pleaded for seven days, crying so hard that he finally wept tears of blood. Seeing Inzan's sincerity and determination, the manager told Gessen, who consented to see the young pilgrim.

Zen master Gessen asked Inzan, "You insistently ask to be allowed to stay here. What do you want to do?"

Inzan replied, "I am only here because the matter of life and death is important, and impermanence is swift."

Gessen retorted, "Here at place there is no big thing to life and no big thing to death. How could it seem that life passes by quickly and death comes swiftly?"

Inzan said, "It is precisely this freedom from life and death that I have been wondering about. Please take pity on me."

Gessen said, "You are young, a mere child. If you really want to practice Zen, you might as well go ahead."

So Inzan joined the congregation, studying day and night without slacking.

Two years later, at the age of twenty-one, Inzan participated in his first session of collective intensive meditation. He felt that he had realized something, and went to tell Gessen.

The master saw that something was different about Inzan and posed a question. "I do not ask about the spoken or the unspoken; try to tell me the answer."

Inzan tried to say something. Gessen remarked, "After all you have fallen into intellectual consciousness," and sent him off.

Inzan went back to the meditation hall in a daze and did nothing but snivel and weep day and night. Everyone laughed at him and called him crazy.

Then one night in the midst of a contemplative trance Inzan suddenly saw through the meaning of "no big thing to life and no big thing to death." He went to tell Gessen, who commented, "You are right, but note that this is just a temporary byway. Do not think this is enough. If you keep on making progress and do not give up, someday you will have your own life."

In the spring of his twenty-sixth year, Inzan left Gessen and went traveling with some companions to visit the distinguished elder Zen masters of Kyoto and western Japan.

Inzan met with the elder masters and questioned them to make sure of his own understanding of Zen. All of the masters admired him and treated him kindly. No one prodded him anymore, so Inzan came to think there were no more enlightened masters in the whole country.

Inzan then left the area. Coming to central Japan, he went to see a Zen master living there. That master appointed Inzan abbot of a local temple.

Now this temple had no patrons, and no fields or gardens. Living contentedly in utter poverty, Inzan sat there for more than ten years.

One day, however, a traveling monk came by the temple with news of Zen master Gasan, a distinguished graduate of Hakuin's school, said to have the foremost eye of wisdom in the land.

Inzan packed his bag that very day and went to Edo, where Gasan was lecturing on *The Blue Cliff Record* to an audience of more than six hundred listeners.

When Inzan arrived, he went right in to see Gasan. The great master stuck out his hand and asked, "Why is this called a hand?" Before Inzan could reply, Gasan now stuck out a foot and said, "Why is this called a foot?" As Inzan tried to make some remark, the great master Gasan clapped his hands and bellowed with laughter. Dumbfounded, Inzan withdrew.

The next day, Inzan went to see Gasan again. The great master said to him, "People who practice Zen today go through the impenetrable koans of the ancients breezily, without ever having done any real work. They versify the koans, or quote them, or add capping phrases, or give answers, all of them running off at the mouth, talking at random.

"For this reason many of them lose the spirit of the Way after they become abbots. Even if they don't run into trouble, none of them can really be teachers. It is truly pitiful.

"If you really want to practice Zen, then cast off everything you have studied and realized up until now and seek enlightenment single-mindedly."

Then Gasan told Inzan to contemplate an advanced koan dealing with his precise problem.

Inzan retreated into a local shrine to meditate, never coming out except for gruel and rice at dawn and noon. After several days like this, all of a sudden one morning he realized the meaning of the koan.

Hurrying back to Gasan, he presented his understanding. The great master was delighted. Meeting with Gasan every day after that, Inzan made a thorough study of the most puzzling stories and attained the inner secrets of Zen. He was then thirty-nine years old.

Later Inzan became a great Zen teacher in his own right, his fame resounding throughout the land. He had numerous distinguished disciples and left a rich spiritual bequest. After his death at the age of sixty-four, the imperial court awarded him the honorific title Zen Teacher, Lamp of Truth, Light of the Nation.

Contentment

Kansan left home when he was nine years old. He had a brilliant mind and studied both Buddhist and Confucian classics. Inspired by one of the books he read, for a time Kansan devoted himself to the study and practice of esoteric Buddhism in western Japan. Later he went to the capital city of Edo, where he perused the massive Buddhist canon.

After nearly two decades of these studies, Kansan finally went to see a Zen teacher. Well versed in Buddhist practices, Kansan mastered the Zen teachings in two years of intensive work.

Subsequently Kansan was sent to take over the abbacy of a temple in southern Japan. When he arrived, he found that drinking and carousing were so common in the area that the temple itself was accustomed to supplying visitors with wine, as if it were a lounge.

On the day that Kansan formally took over the abbacy of the temple, he destroyed every single wine jar, ashtray, and serving table. After that, guests were treated with a single cup of plain tea.

Three years later, Kansan retired. He disappeared into the mountains, putting a sign over the door of his hut that simply said, "Content."

The Sound of One Hand Clapping

When Taigen was a young man, he heard that the great Zen master Inzan was not only an enlightened Buddhist but an accomplished scholar of ancient Chinese history. Traveling directly to the Zen master's abode in provincial central

Japan, Taigen asked to be allowed to study Zen with him and also to hear him lecture on a historical classic.

Inzan said to Taigen, "If you can hear the sound of one hand clapping, then and only then will I lecture on history to you."

Now Taigen was really excited. He plunged into deep meditation in order to solve the mystery of one hand clapping. To help his concentration, sometimes he would sit in a deep tub, and sometimes he would climb up into the mountain behind his hut to sit on a boulder. At times he would sit until dawn, not even realizing the whole night had passed.

At this time, Taigen was staying in a hermitage several miles from Inzan's place. Nevertheless, every day he would go to seek guidance, even when the road was several feet deep in snow. On numerous occasions in very deep snow he collapsed on the way, overcome by the cold, and had to be rescued by villagers.

Later Inzan moved to another temple, and Taigen followed him there to continue his apprenticeship. One night, after many more severe trials at the hands of the master, Taigen finally experienced great enlightenment.

Nature Lover

Once there was a baron who was extremely fond of chrysanthemums. He had the whole rear garden of his mansion planted with them, and spent a lot of time and effort cultivating them.

In fact, the baron paid more attention to the care of his chrysanthemums than to his wife and concubines. Many of his retainers were punished for inadvertently breaking off a blossom. In short, the baron's passion for chrysanthemums made life miserable for everyone around him.

On one occasion, when a certain retainer accidentally broke off a blossom, he was ordered into confinement by the furious baron. Enraged by this treatment, the retainer resolved to disembowel himself in protest, according to the traditional warrior code.

Now it so happened that Zen master Sengai heard of this and hastened to intervene, preventing the retainer from committing suicide over such an affair.

Not content with a temporary measure, Sengai resolved to effect a permanent solution. One rainy night when the chrysanthemums were in full bloom, Sengai sneaked into the baron's garden with a sickle and cut down every single chrysanthemum.

Hearing a strange sound from the garden, the baron looked out and saw someone there. Rushing out wielding his sword in great alarm, he demanded to know what Sengai was doing.

The Zen master calmly replied, "Even weeds like this eventually become rank if they are not cut."

Now the baron realized how wrong he had been. It was like awakening from a dream. From that time onward, he no longer raised chrysanthemums.

An Innocent

Yamamoto Yasuo was a scholar of ancient Japanese literature and an expert in native poetry. Lamenting the decline of the imperial cultus, he wrote a book called *The Reality of the Gods* and killed himself in protest.

A wealthy man of social standing, Yamamoto left five children behind when he died, four sons and one daughter. His eldest son, a free-spirited youth, had no desire to inherit the family fortune. Giving up everything, he left home to study Zen, changing his name to Great Fool.

At the age of twenty-two, the young mendicant went

traveling to look for a teacher. Finding a Zen master who could guide him, he mastered the teaching in a few years of intensive work.

Then he went traveling again, calling on Zen masters all over the land, seeking further enlightenment. It was more than twenty years before he returned to his native province, where he built a hut. He was so poor that he wore a robe of patches, lived on gruel, and had no utensils save a single bowl, which he used for every purpose from grinding bean paste and cooking gruel to washing his hands and feet.

This Zen master loved to play with children. Wherever he went, he would gather a group to play kickball or hide-and-seek. Once when the master was in a game of hide-and-seek, the children went home, leaving him where he was. He stood still with his eyes closed till nightfall, when someone finally asked him what he was doing. He replied that he was playing hide-and-seek with the children and waiting for someone to come find him. He didn't even realize they had played a joke on him.

Once someone asked him why he liked to play with children. The master said, "I like their genuineness, their lack of falsehood." As a famous calligrapher, he was often approached with requests for writing, but he used to refuse if it didn't feel right to him. Whenever children asked him to write something, however, he would always be glad to take up his brush.

The master used to tell people, "There are three things I very much dislike: the poetry of poets, the writing of writers, and the cuisine of cooks."

The First Stone

Once Zen master Dairyo was invited to a feast at the home of a wealthy landowner. Many other Buddhist monks were also present.

Someone in the household decided to play a joke on the monks. All of them were served with fish flesh, which Buddhist monks and nuns were forbidden to eat.

All of the monks at the feast abstained from the fish flesh except Zen master Dairyo, who ate it all, as if he didn't know what it was.

One of the monks surreptitiously pulled the Zen master's sleeve and said, "That's fish flesh!"

Dairyo looked the monk in the eye and retorted, "So how do you know what fish flesh is?"

Reality and Fakery

Zōbō pursued only literary studies before someone warned him that was not the way to ultimate truth. Then he went to a Zen master and learned to contemplate emptiness.

It took a long time for Zōbō to attain realization. Eventually, he got to the point where he was so absorbed in concentration that he forgot to eat and sleep.

One night as he was sitting quietly, unawares Zōbō fell asleep from exhaustion. When his Zen teacher struck him to wake him up, all at once he realized enlightenment.

Zōbō was twenty-three years old at the time. His teacher was strict and did not acknowledge people easily. Zōbō continued intensive study for over ten more years and finally completed the Great Work.

As a teacher in his own right, Zōbō was single-minded. Unconcerned with social conventions, he devoted himself solely to teaching Zen. Lamenting the degeneration of Zen schools, he roundly criticized imitation Zen masters and ignorant Zen followers.

Zōbō was also uncompromising in his private teaching and would not admit superficial understanding. Many seekers came to his school, but very few ever passed.

Zōbō was scarcely over sixty years old when he passed away in 1840. On the brink of death, he wrote a final verse:

> Zōbō at sixty! Here's my real state:
> Where eight clouds are standing, I piss at the sky.
> It's a wonder, and a pity too,
> I didn't kill all the imitation Zen in the world.

After Zōbō's death, the emperor of Japan titled him Zen Master, Spiritual Mirror Shining Alone.

Respect

Fūgai met more than ten Zen teachers, but his own mind was so sharp and free that no one could equal him. Finally he met the redoubtable Genrō the Wolf and attained great enlightenment at a single saying of the great Zen master. After he mastered the inner teachings, Fūgai left Genrō and disappeared into anonymity to mature his spiritual development.

Among Fūgai's successors was Tanzan, one of the outstanding masters of early modern times. Tanzan was also unusually sharp, and he saw through many of the Zen preachers of the day in his youth before he met master Fūgai.

Unlike his teacher Genrō before him, Zen master Fūgai was outwardly warm and gentle. Tanzan, in contrast, was a burly, virile man, temperamentally more like his spiritual grandfather Genrō. When Tanzan first met Fūgai, he took the mild gentility of the master as a sign of weakness and inwardly scorned him. Perceiving this, Fūgai suddenly posed a question so piercing that Tanzan broke out in a sweat all over his body, completely at a loss for something to say. Now Tanzan recognized Fūgai's unobtrusive mastery and became a true disciple.

Once Tanzan saw a painting of a tiger made by Fūgai. He remarked, "This tiger is like a cat, but even so it has its own inviolable majesty."

Plumbing the Source

Even as a child, Kokan wished to avoid the constraints of worldly entanglements. He was only seven years old when he left home to join Buddhist orders. He was initiated and given the precepts by the great Zen master Tōrei, who had been Hakuin's disciple. Within a few months, young Kokan was already capable of reciting scriptures, Zen poetry, and the recorded sayings of ancient masters.

When Kokan was nine years old, his mentor instructed him to pay a courtesy call on his parents. Traveling alone over the mountain path, Kokan slipped and fell into the river running through the valley.

Removing his robe, Kokan laid it out to dry by the side of the path, then sat on a boulder, stark naked, waiting for the robe to dry. Presently he fell asleep from exhaustion.

After a time a woodcutter passing by saw the sleeping boy and woke him up. "You're a traveling monk, aren't you?" he asked Kokan. "Why are you in such a state?"

Young Kokan told the woodcutter the truth of the matter. Then the woodcutter said, "It's almost nightfall. You'll never get where you're going today. Head back for the nearest village right away; I'll even escort you there."

Kokan laughed and said, "If I'm going to be a man, how can I turn back after having come this far?" Then he got up, put on his robe, and stalked off, finally to reach home in the middle of the night. His parents were very much surprised, but they took it in stride, remarking, "Your teacher has guts, letting you make the journey alone! Good thing you had the guts to do it!"

When Kokan was twenty, Tōrei sent him to see Zen master Gasan. Gasan told Kokan to hear the sound of one hand clapping.

Now Kokan went to work contemplating the sound of one hand. His concentrated doubt was so intense that felt as if he were carrying a heavy burden up a steep hill.

At this time it was the dead of winter, and the weather was extremely cold. Since Kokan had nothing but a single robe, Gasan took pity on him and asked one of the lay patrons to give him some padded clothing. Kokan accepted it as a courtesy but would not put it on.

Kokan also ignored the many cultural sites of the eastern capital and refused to go on sight-seeing tours with the other monks. "I have not yet mastered myself," he would say. "What leisure have I to go sight-seeing?"

Then one day as he was walking around the edge of the yard in meditation, all of a sudden Kokan experienced a great enlightenment.

When he told Gasan what he had realized, the elder master tested him with several koans. It turned out that Kokan still had some obstruction. Gasan said, "Although your entry into enlightenment has been ecstatic, you should still examine the root source of the sound of one hand in every detail."

After this, Kokan refined his practice and focused his energies tremendously. He had once asked Gasan who he should follow to complete his Zen studies after Gasan's death, and the old master had recommended Inzan. Now Kokan went to Inzan and worked intensively on cultivating thorough refinement.

Over a long period of time he attained all of the inner secrets of Zen and finished the Great Work. Inzan gave him formal recognition of his mastery and sent him to look after a hermitage. There Kokan spent sixteen years living in poverty and polishing his practice of Zen.

During that interval he often experienced awakenings. Once he had penetrated deeply into the root source of it all, he finally got to see that there was a special higher mystic function in the school of Hakuin, and he attained extraordinary freedom in his everyday experience. After that he taught people according to their individual potentials, and many benefited from his advice.

Like Hakuin, Gasan, and other great Zen masters, Kokan declined the honor of abbacy at a major monastery, preferring to work inconspicuously with sincere seekers only. He also returned a present of gold that had been given to him by a baron, saying he had not practiced Zen to win any prizes.

One year, the crops failed in the central seaboard provinces, and famines ensued among the peasants. Kokan prepared gruel to feed the people who were fleeing starvation, begging along the road. They say that he helped an extremely large number of people in this manner.

As Kokan was nearing death, his foremost disciple asked him for a final verse. He hollered, "My final verse fills the universe! Why bother with pen and paper!"

The disciple said, "Even so, please release yet another expression, a statement of even greater fulfillment, to leave to future generations."

Kokan then smiled and wrote,

> *Seventy-four years*
> *bumping west and bumping east.*
> *The last word?*
> *Shh! Shh!*

Kokan used to guide people by getting them to find out "the root source of the sound of one hand clapping." He was a strict Zen teacher and rarely gave anyone approval. When he died in 1843, he left only a few successors to carry on his work.

Three Kinds of Mendicants

Gettan used to say, "There are three kinds of mendicants. First are those who teach others. Second are those who maintain the sanctuaries. Third are the rice bags and clothes hangers. Descendants of the Zen founder should take complete awareness for their sanctuary and teach others to perpetuate the life of wisdom of the Buddhas. As for those who are no more than rice bags and clothes hangers, they are criminals in Buddhism."

Look into Your Mind

Kakushin went to China in the middle of the thirteenth century to study Zen. There he met a famous Zen master who asked him, "What is your name?"

Kakushin told the Zen master his name.

Noting that the name Kakushin means "Awakening the Mind" or "Awake Mind," the master wrote a verse for the pilgrim:

> *Mind is Buddha,*
> *Buddha is mind:*
> *Mind and Buddha,*
> *being such, are there*
> *throughout all time.*

After Kakushin's return to Japan, Emperor Kameyama heard of his Zen mastery and summoned him to teach in one of the imperial temples. Later the emperor also invited the master to the palace to ask him about Zen.

The master's profound discourse, immense intelligence, and uninhibited eloquence impressed Emperor Kameyama beyond anything he had ever known.

Realizing the exceptional quality of Zen Buddhism, the emperor converted the imperial residence into a Zen sanctuary.

The next emperor, Go-Uta, also invited Kakushin to a special imperial villa to teach Zen. The master said, "The Buddhas understand mind; ordinary people misunderstand mind. The source of all Buddhas is one; the realms of misunderstanding and understanding divide. Without depending on another power, you can know by inherent capacity. If you want to arrive at Buddhahood, you must look into your own mind."

Undistracted

Utame was only fifteen years old when she first received instruction from an enlightened Zen nun, who taught her how to look into the innermost self.

Utame plunged into meditation day and night, paying no attention to anything else. Even when she was at her mirror putting on makeup, she was inwardly looking into the essence of mind. Sometimes she would become so absorbed that she would forget what she was doing and just sit there silently.

Now her parents, who had no idea what lay behind their daughter's strange behavior, began to think she might be suffering from depression or heading for a nervous breakdown. They tried to get her to go out to the theater and take trips to scenic places, but Utame had no desire for any of these diversions.

Finally one day her efforts came to fruition, and the young woman's mind opened up in great enlightenment.

Later Utame married and bore four children, two sons and two daughters. Her husband had the misfortune to go bankrupt, so Utame took up needlework to help support the family. She lived to be more than seventy years old, eventually passing away one day in a state of serene repose.

Beating a Bully

Descendant of a famous warrior, Butsugai was fierce and courageous. Although he entered Buddhist orders when he was only twelve years old, Butsugai mastered archery, horsemanship, and all the other traditional martial arts. Immensely strong, he could punch a hole in just about anything. Because of his physical power, he was called the Monk with Punching Power.

In the middle of the nineteenth century, Japan was rocked by civil disturbances. At this time, a certain warrior band called the New Elite came to Kyoto, hoping to rise to power in a new national order. Rowdy and self-indulgent, this group of warriors became the terror of the townspeople.

One day Butsugai was walking along the street in Kyoto, when he happened to pass by the place where the New Elite were quartered. Drawn by the sound of bamboo swords clashing, Butsugai found himself looking in through the window.

Presently a few warriors came out, angrily demanding to know what Butsugai was doing there. He apologized, saying he was only a monk who had just come out of the mountains. The warriors decided to have some fun with this monk, so they challenged him to duel with them. "Anyone spying on us here," they insisted, "must know something about martial arts."

Butsugai couldn't refuse. He went into the training room

with the warriors, who took up bamboo swords one after another to face the ragged monk.

Without evincing the slightest alarm, Butsugai took his iron ceremonial scepter and smashed down the sword of each attacker. In a matter of minutes, the Buddhist monk had overcome several dozen men.

Now the leader of the warrior band picked up a spear and stepped forward. "Your skills are too much for these young knights," he said to Butsugai, "but now I, Kondō Isamu, am challenging you to a match."

Butsugai appeared to be terrified. Falling to the ground in a gesture of utmost humility, he said, "Kondō Isamu! I have heard of you! They call you a genius of the martial arts. A wandering monk like me could hardly hope to stand up to someone like you. Please let me go."

Further emboldened, the warrior refused to withdraw his challenge. He pressed Butsugai until the monk, unable to avoid a contest any longer, he again took up his iron scepter and stood facing the warrior chief.

Kondō said to Butsugai, "You need a weapon. Take a bamboo sword, or a wooden spear, or whatever you want."

Butsugai replied, "As a Buddhist monk, I am not supposed to pick up weapons. This ceremonial scepter will do."

The warrior would not let the monk off. He insisted that Butsugai use a weapon.

Ever resourceful, the Zen monk reached into his pouch and took out a pair of wooden bowls. Gripping one in each hand, he said to the warrior, "Okay, go ahead! Just try to spear me if you can!"

This insolence infuriated the warrior chief. Now he was determined to knock the monk down with a single thrust. Gripping his spear, he looked for an opening in the monk's unusual defense.

The warrior stood motionless and unblinking for nearly half an hour, unable to see a way to attack. Then he must have thought he noticed an opening, for all of a sudden he thrust his spear with every ounce of power and rage he could muster, intending to shatter the monk's rib cage.

Slipping the attack with great agility, Butsugai immediately caught the spear between the two bowls, holding it fast in a viselike grip.

Try as he might, the warrior chief could not wrest his spear free from the clamp of the monk's begging bowls. He pushed and pulled this way and that, until he was soaked in perspiration.

After a good long while of this, Butsugai suddenly released the spear, along with a piercing shout. The warrior tumbled backward, his spear flying twenty or thirty feet behind him.

Awed and humbled, the warrior chief bowed to Butsugai and said, "Your skills are truly outstanding, way beyond me. Who are you?"

"I am a wandering monk named Butsugai," the Zen Buddhist replied.

"So you're the famous Monk with a Punch!" exclaimed the warrior chief, who now treated his erstwhile opponent with greatest respect.

After this the name of Butsugai was heard throughout the ancient capital.

When Butsugai finished his Zen study, he went into seclusion to mature his enlightenment. Before long, however, people who had heard of him began to gather around him in great numbers to study, either Zen or the martial arts.

There was a renowned swordsman who met Butsugai once when he was a young man on a journey to study martial arts. Calling on Butsugai, the young samurai asked for some teaching.

Butsugai asked him, "What have you come here for?"

The young man replied, "I have come to die at the teacher's fists."

Butsugai considered this a remarkable answer and let the young swordsman stay for a while. Butsugai presented him with a verse, saying,

> *Even the power of the Howling Spirit—*
> *a single layer of mosquito netting.*

By meditating on this verse, the swordsman later related when he had become renowned throughout western Japan, he attained inner understanding of the hidden essence of jujitsu, the "gentle art."

Butsugai became so famous that many of the major barons of western Japan invited him to their domains, offering him the choicest of temples for his residence. Butsugai refused all of them, remaining in a poor temple until he died, wearing old clothing and living contentedly with a bare subsistence, never seeking anything else.

The Mind of Sages

In 1262, Hōjō Tokiyori, regent of the Shōgun, went to see Zen master Funei. He announced, "Recently I have perceived that which is neither impermanent nor permanent."

The Zen master said, "Zen study only aims at perception of essential nature. If you attain perception of essential nature, you will understand everything."

The regent asked, "Please teach me a method."

The Zen master responded, "There are no two Ways in the world; sages do not have two minds. If you know the mind of sages, you will find that it is the inherent essence that is the root source of your own self."

The Art of Art

Zen master Tetsuō was so famous for his brush painting that many people came to him just to study art. He always used to tell prospective students, "You must remember the saying, 'If you want to avoid depending on society, don't let criticism and praise disturb your heart.' When you can cultivate your art without leaving any mundanity at all in your chest, then mind and technique will naturally mature, and you will eventually be able to arrive at the subtleties. This is the way out of darkness into light."

Once a distinguished Confucian scholar and statesman came to visit Tetsuō. Observing the Zen master executing a painting, the scholar noted that every move of the master's arm and brush was in conformity with the classical principles of calligraphy.

When he remarked upon this, the Zen master explained, "In terms of correctness of mind, calligraphy and painting are one. When I make a painting, if so much as one cane of bamboo or one leaf on a tree is even slightly off from the way the stroke should be, I tear the whole thing up and throw it away, then put aside my brush, sit quietly, and clarify my mind."

Zen Literature

Kaigan championed the neglected study of Buddhist and Zen literature in the middle of the nineteenth century. Many people thought he was just a scholar, not realizing that he was an enlightened Zen master.

Kaigan first studied scriptural Buddhism with the great

Zen master Sengai. Later he studied Zen meditation with Seisetsu and Tankai. Kaigan completed his Zen study with Tankai and was recognized as a successor.

At one point Kaigan went to Kyoto to study at the academies of the other schools of Buddhism. Disturbed by what he found, Kaigan wrote,

> *At the Fifth Avenue bridge,*
> *I turn my head and look;*
> *east, west, south, north,*
> *ignorant monks are many.*

Later on, Zen master Dokuon explained, "People of the time all considered Kaigan to be widely learned, with a powerful memory. And that is indeed true.

"However, he also had three Zen teachers and found out the innermost secrets of Zen, finally receiving the seal of approval from Zen master Tankai. People of his time thought Kaigan was a teacher of doctrinal Buddhism, but that was not his reality.

"What Kaigan was worried about was that there were many Zen followers with sterile intellects and few who understood the principles of the Teaching. It was because of this that he concentrated on preaching literary Zen, in order to develop and guide young seekers.

"Kaigan's attention was focused on rescuing people from the decadence of the times. He didn't have time to pay any mind to other things. That is precisely what made him great."

Elegance

Zen master Tetsuō wrote the following words on his fireplace screen:

"Be upright and honest, conscious of the principles of

nature, compassionate and generous toward others, free from greed, contented. Carry out your everyday affairs correctly, without error. Take care of things without being attached to them.

"To be free from ordinary feelings about mundane objects is called the elegance of the ancients. We do not find this among the fashionable people of today. For this reason I close my door and do not admit visitors.

"I have no lofty reputation, nor do I wish an exalted name. In order to live as I will, I feign incompetence, only wishing to fulfill what is naturally so. I am no one's teacher. People who try to learn from me are crazy. That is because they study my craziness and do not study my heart."

Resolve

Settan became a monk when he was only ten years old. One day he decided to go traveling to find a real guide, and he asked his mentor permission to leave. His mentor refused.

Determined to find the Way, Settan decided to go without telling anyone. Hanging a note on the temple gate saying, "Unless I attain the Way, I will never enter this gateway again," he left.

Finding his way to the congregation of Zen master Tōrin, Settan sat in meditation day and night. Tōrin was one of the few enlightened teachers left in those days, and his method was stern and unpredictable.

One day Settan finally decided he had no more time to waste. Climbing up to the top of a building, he vowed that he would not come down alive unless he attained enlightenment that night.

Sitting in deep meditation all through the night, by dawn

Settan still had not broken through. Getting up in disgust, he went to the railing to jump off the building to his death.

All of a sudden, just as he was about to step over, he heard a cock crow. At that moment Settan's mind opened up, and he was greatly enlightened.

Overwhelmed with joy, Settan hurried to the teacher. When master Tōrin saw him, at once he affirmed, "You've broken through!"

The Good Heart

The layman Sasaki Doppo studied Zen with Ganseki. He later recounted how he had asked his teacher, "What is Buddha?" Ganseki replied, "The good heart is Buddha."

The layman added, "What is most basic in the human world is a good heart. Therefore the normal mind is called the Way."

He also expressed these ideas in a verse on Shinto, the Spirit Religion:

> *The defilement known as taboo*
> *is made up by the human mind;*
> *people who know the divine mind*
> *are themselves divine.*

He also wrote,

> *The sun my eyes,*
> *the sky my face,*
> *my breath the wind,*
> *mountains and rivers*
> *turn out to be me.*

A Poet

Jōsō the Buddhist monk was a student of the famous haiku master Bashō. His religious practices and attainments were generally kept secret, and he was mostly known only as a poet.

Originally a samurai, Jōsō was a hereditary retainer of a certain barony. As the eldest son, he was due to inherit his father's estate, but he was devoted to his stepmother and arranged for her son, his younger half-brother, to succeed to the family inheritance in his stead.

In feudal Japan, it was not possible to make such a decision arbitrarily. Deliberately wounding his right hand, Jōsō retired from official service on the grounds of disability, claiming he could not wield a sword. Unfit to be a warrior, he was no longer qualified to become head of a samurai house.

That was how the poet Jōsō freed himself from worldly affairs to become a Zen monk. After the death of his teacher Bashō, he secluded himself in a cave for three years, where he wrote out an entire Buddhist scripture on pebbles, one Chinese character to a pebble, and piled them up into a traditional "scripture mound." He also wrote a book of advice for both priests and ordinary people; although it was full of high-minded thoughts, he called it *The Layabout Book*.

In commemoration of the occasion of his retirement from the world, Jōsō composed this poem in formal Chinese style:

> *Having carried its house*
> *on its back for years,*
> *a snail turns into a slug*
> *and thereby gains its freedom.*
> *In the burning house,*
> *his greatest fear*
> *was that his spit would dry:*
> *Now seeking the rain of religion,*
> *he enters a forested hill.*

The Ex-Abbot

At one time, Yūren was the abbot of a certain temple in Edo, the capital city of the Third Shogunate. He was so inspired by his readings of biographies of eminent Buddhists of ancient times, however, that he decided to leave his post to do further work on his own spiritual development.

Leaving a letter claiming to be ill and unable to manage his duties as abbot, Yūren traveled alone and in secret to Kyoto, the ancient capital and center of traditional culture.

Staying in various places in the Kyoto area, Yūren never accumulated any possessions whatsoever throughout his life. Morning and night he chanted Buddhist invocations, and he composed poetry in his free time between religious exercises.

Yūren did not own a single book of poetry. He had no idea how to adorn his language and just expressed his thoughts. Yet for that very reason his poetry had a quality of genuine directness that set it apart from the crowd.

Once he wrote a verse for a caption on a picture of a beauty looking at a skull:

> *Now you surely*
> *won't pick up the mirror*
> *you've been looking in*
> *morning and night,*
> *seeing that this*
> *is your real appearance.*

He wrote several poems with single letters for titles, among them this one:

> *Looking over the fields,*
> *I see the unknown smoke*
> *rising again today.*
> *Whose body will be*
> *the kindling tomorrow?*

This poem is on geese flying past the moon:

> *Though the geese*
> *go flying by crying,*
> *my heart stays*
> *on the autumn night's moon.*

Once a certain priest who had been living in borrowed quarters at a temple accidentally caused it to burn down. On this occasion Yūren wrote,

> *Use such an occasion to test*
> *the ultimate unshakability*
> *of the usually immutable mind.*

At the request of someone going into the service of a noble, Yūren wrote,

> *When you're headed for good fortune,*
> *don't forget to remember*
> *that the world is inconstant.*

This was Yūren's song to the spirits:

> *Though I've nothing to ask*
> *for the self I've abandoned,*
> *let me pray to the spirits*
> *for the path of the heart.*

The Original Religion

The high priest Tsū-an was a commoner by birth. He was a selfless man, upright and honest. Not only did he study Zen, he was also well versed in all the genteel arts of the tea ceremony, incense compounding, flower arranging, and so on.

Tsū-an also studied medicine. Although his teacher specialized in moxacautery, he himself decided to travel around the country to examine and test the effects of various hot springs. He located two places where the water was outstanding, but they were in remote areas, so he developed a method of treating ordinary water that would produce similar effects. He had this formula printed and distributed it as an act of charity.

Tsū-an's mental and physical vigor did not decline as he grew old. He was a delightful and refreshing person. Once a housewife in his locality was sick for years, tormented by a ghost. During that time, whenever a physician would come, she would go wild and shout abuse, such that no doctor would dare approach her. When Tsū-an came, however, even if the woman was in her sickroom, she would become aware of his presence the instant he crossed the threshold. She would be terribly frightened and would submit docilely to his examination.

Tsū-an died in the year 1750 at the age of eighty. At noon of the day he passed away, he felt his own pulse and declared that his life would end before the hour was up. As it turned out, he actually died within the hour, leaving behind this parting verse:

> *The original religion*
> *is realized without beginning.*
> *As my eyes close forever,*
> *my essence is true emptiness.*

Curing Zen Sickness

When Zen master Hakuin was a young man, like most people he attained partial insight before realizing complete liberation. He therefore determined to make an intensive effort to achieve a thorough breakthrough.

After a month of strenuous exertion, Hakuin reached the

point where he would forget to eat and sleep. Finally his heart and lungs were adversely affected, and he had a constant ringing in his ears and chills in his feet.

Becoming enfeebled and suffering from anxiety and hallucinations, Hakuin was alarmed; he sought medical treatment, but to no avail. Finally someone told him about a man called Hakuyūshi, "the Pure Hermit," who lived in a mountain cave east of Kyoto.

Hakuyūshi was believed to be over two hundred years old. Outwardly he appeared to be an imbecile. Living deep in the mountains, he did not like to have visitors. Whenever anyone came looking for him, he invariably ran away. The local people considered him a wizard. He was an expert on astronomy and was also deeply versed in medical arts. If people sincerely sought answers from him, he would sometimes say something, which on reflection would always prove to be of great benefit.

Hakuin set off for Kyoto to see Hakuyūshi in the winter of 1710. Entering deeply into the mountains on the eastern outskirts of the ancient capital, he asked directions from woodcutters. Plowing through the snow, walking along the crags, after much difficulty he came to a cave with a reed blind hung at the entrance.

Looking in through the gaps in the blind, Hakuin saw Hakuyūshi sitting there with his eyes closed. He had dark hair reaching to his knees and a healthy ruddy complexion. On a desk were three books: a Confucian classic, a Taoist text, and a Buddhist scripture. There were no utensils or bedding anywhere in sight. The whole atmosphere was one of purity and transcendence, beyond the human realm.

Timidly and nervously, Hakuin told the hermit about his symptoms and asked for his help. At first Hakuyūshi feigned ignorance and excused himself, but on Hakuin's earnest and insistent pleas he at length agreed to check his vital signs.

After making his examination, the hermit frowned and said, "You're done for. Excess in meditation has produced these grave symptoms. I'm afraid no one could cure you with the usual treatments of acupuncture, moxacautery, and medication. You have been maimed by inner contemplation. If you do not strive to build up the positive effects of inner contemplation, you will never get well. This is what is meant by the saying, 'One who falls on the ground must get up from the ground.'"

Hakuin said he would give up Zen meditation so that he might be cured of his affliction. Hakuyūshi smiled and said, "Zen meditation is nothing special. In general, meditation is correct meditation when there is no 'meditation.' Too much meditation is wrong meditation. You became sick because of too much meditation; now you should use nonmeditation to heal yourself."

Then the hermit instructed Hakuin in genuinely correct methods of pure meditation, citing Buddhist scriptures and Zen lore. He also mentioned a marvelous technique for relief of mental stress and fatigue, which he said was found in ancient literature. Hakuin asked him about the details.

Hakuyūshi explained, "When you feel ill during concentration exercises, you should rouse the mind to perform the following visualization. Imagine a ball of soft, pure, fragrant butter on top of your head. Its flavor subtly refreshes the whole head, then gradually flows down to the shoulders chest, lungs, liver, stomach, and intestines, and down the backbone to the hips. Now the congestion in your chest will flow downward like water, going down through the body, down the legs to the bottom of the feet, where it will stop.

"Then imagine that the penetrating moisture of the remaining flow accumulates and that all kinds of aromatic medicines are blended together in a tonic that soaks and permeates the body from the umbilical region downward.

"When doing this visualization, it is all just a manifestation of mind, so you will smell an exquisite fragrance and experience a subtle, soft tactile sensation in your body. Your body and mind will be harmonious and comfortable. Congestion will dissolve, your viscera will be in tune, your skin will become lustrous, and you will gain a great deal of energy and strength.

"If you persist in this, you will become physically well and mentally elevated. Whether the effect takes place slowly or quickly depends entirely on how diligent you are.

"In the past I had many illnesses, much worse than yours. By using this method, however, I was able to relieve most of my chronic ailments within a month. Now I live in these mountains without fear of cold and without suffering hunger. All this is due to the power of that visualization."

Hakuin left after receiving these instructions. After three years of practice, his sickness was cured. Not only was he relieved of illness, he was able to penetrate his doubt as well. He attained great ecstasy several times and had numerous blissful insights. He lived to a ripe old age, attributing his health and strength to the residual effects of the techniques he had learned from the hermit Hakuyūshi.

Zen in Daily Life

Man-an wrote to a government official: "People in all walks of life have all sorts of things to attend to. How could they have the leisure to sit silently all day in quiet contemplation? Here there are Zen teachers who have not managed to cultivate this sitting meditation concentration; they teach deliberate seclusion and quietude, avoiding population centers, stating that 'intensive meditation concentration cannot be attained in the midst of professional work, business, and labor,' thus causing students to apply their minds mistakenly.

"People who listen to this kind of talk consequently think of Zen as something that is hard to do and hard to practice, so they give up the inspiration to cultivate Zen, abandon the source and try to escape, time and again becoming like lowly migrant workers. This is truly lamentable. Even if they have a deep aspiration due to some cause in the past, they get to where they neglect their jobs and lose their social virtues for the sake of the Way.

"As an ancient said, if people today were as eager for enlightenment as they are to embrace their lovers, then no matter how busy their professional lives might be, and no matter how luxurious their dwellings, they would not fail to attain continuous concentration leading to appearance of the Great Wonder.

"Many people of both ancient and modern times have awakened to the Way and seen essential nature in the midst of activity. All beings in all times and places are manifestations of one mind. When the mind is aroused, all sorts of things arise; when the mind is quiet, all things are quiet. When the one mind is unborn, all things are blameless. For this reason, even if you stay in quiet and serene places deep in the mountains and sit silently in quiet contemplation, as long as the road of the mind-monkey's horse of conceptualization is not cut off, you will only be wasting time.

"The Third Patriarch of Zen said, 'If you try to stop movement and resort to stillness, that stopping will cause even more movement.' If you try to seek true suchness by erasing random thoughts, you will belabor your vital spirit, diminish your mental energy, and make yourself sick. Not only that, you will become oblivious or distracted and fall into a pit of bewilderment."

No Chaff

Once Zen master Settan was invited to a certain monastery to lecture on a Zen classic. The baron of the province attended the talk, seated behind a screen.

When Settan got up onto the lecture stand and saw the screen, he shouted, "Who is this impudent fellow, listening from behind a screen? There is no chaff at my lectures, so there is no need for a sieve! Unless you get that winnowing basket out of here, there will be no talk today."

Everyone in the audience went pale. The baron was extremely embarrassed. Apologizing to the Zen master, he had the screen removed and sat there listening to the talk along with everyone else.

Guidelines

Settan once wrote a set of guidelines for Zen monasteries: "An ancient said that Zen study requires three essentials. One is a great root of faith. The second is a great feeling of wonder. The third is great determination. If one of these is lacking, you are like a tripod missing a leg.

"Here I have no special stipulations. I only require that you clearly recognize that everyone has an essential nature that can be perceived, and that there is an essential truth that everyone can penetrate; only then will your determination continue. And there are sayings at which to wonder. If people go off half aware and half awakened, they cannot really succeed in Zen. It is imperative to be careful and thoroughgoing."

Teacher of a Nation

Shōichi traveled to China in 1235, where he learned the secrets of Zen from one of the great masters of the time. After returning to Japan in 1241, Shōichi began to teach Zen in the rural south. In 1243 he was invited to Kyoto, the imperial capital, by the distinguished courtier Fujiwara Michiie. He died in 1280 at the age of seventy-eight.

When Shōichi met Emperor Gosaga in 1245, he presented him with a copy of the *Source Mirror Record,* an immense compendium of Buddhist teachings compiled by a famous Chinese Zen master of the tenth century. The emperor used to read this book whenever he had free time. When he finished, he wrote in the back of the text, "Having received this book from Master Shōichi, we have now seen essential nature."

When the courtier Fujiwara Michiie asked him for Zen instruction, Shōichi said, "It is a matter of having decisive willpower, so that you can be the master in the middle of all kinds of differences and distinctions."

Lotus in the Mud

Torio Tokuan said, "Do not consider yourself elevated in comparison to ordinary people. Those who are commonplace just rise and fall on the road of fame and profit, without practicing the Way or following the Way.

"They are only to be pitied, not despised or resented. Do not give rise to judgmental thoughts by comparing yourself to them; do not give rise to ideas of higher and lower.

"This is the attitude needed to enter the Way of the sages and saints, buddhas and bodhisattvas. Therefore we place ourselves in the state of ordinary people, assimilating to the ordinary, while our will is on the Way, and we investigate its wonders."

The Great Death

Itachi Jitoku was a knight in the employ of a certain barony when he ran afoul of a highly placed bureaucrat by speaking out too frankly and directly. As a result, he was relieved of duty and imprisoned in a castle.

For thirteen years Jitoku sat in one room, indifferent to the privations of captivity. The rules of the barony allowed prisoners no reading material save Buddhist texts, so Jitoku borrowed a copy of the whole canon and began to read it through, passing his time absorbed in the ocean of Buddhist teachings.

At length Jitoku was pardoned and restored to his former status. Now over sixty years old, he went to see the noted Zen master Ekkei to deepen his understanding.

As soon as Jitoku entered the door, the Zen master jumped on him and punched him.

The knight was enraged. No one had ever struck him before, not even his father. He went to Dokuon, another Zen master, and angrily declared his intention to challenge Ekkei to a duel to the death.

Seeing that the knight was serious, Zen master Dokuon smiled and said, "Old Ekkei has always been willing to give his life for the sake of the truth. Even if you kill him, I'm sure he won't resent it. However, he was simply trying to help you. You don't know what power he has in his fist! If you kill him for no good reason, it will be no more than an assassination. Why not take a step back and try to achieve a breakthrough? I'm sure you will see how kind Ekkei was to you."

Feeling somewhat mollified, Jitoku took Dokuon's advice

and went home to meditate. For three days and three nights he concentrated all of his energy, until he finally attained the Great Death of Zen, in which the barriers of the ego are dissolved.

Returning to Dokuon, Jitoku said, "Now I realize that Ekkei was still pulling his punches. If I had let him beat me to death, no doubt I'd have made an even greater break-through!"

Zen and the World

When Zen master Gisan was given a title of honor by the emperor of Japan in 1866, he responded with these poems:

HUMANITY AND LAW
Self-help and helping others:
this trance of mine
is dutiful at home, loyal in public,
never obscured in daily affairs.

THE BENEFIT OF BUDDHISM FOR NATIONS
Do not kill, and life will be sufficient;
do not steal, and goods will be plenty.
How excellent the moral teachings:
they enrich nations and stabilize families.

PROTECTING THE NATION
Whatever is bad, do not do;
whatever is good, carry it out:
then above and below will harmonize,
the good and the bad won't compete.